Journey to Reality

Journey to Reality

JEAN INGLIS ALLISON

Published by Jean Inglis Allison
2308 Durston Road
Bozeman, MT 59718

ISBN: 978-1-4243-3573-2

Printed in the United States of America

Dedicated to

Elizabeth Clare Prophet

Contents

My Philosophy of Life

Jean Inglis Thayer
January 21, 1946

*I*t doesn't come out of space, it's developed from your soul; you don't copy it from other lives nor books, it's the way you try to shape your life.

Philosophy is a big word, and for thousands of years people of every race and creed in some manner or form have described it in their own way. Some of the greatest men of all time have given us basic ideas on which to form good lives that they have so greatly lived, though they were not perfect.

My arrangement isn't fancy, my vocabulary poor; yet I'm going to write on paper the ideas I wish to base my life upon. You must understand I can't accomplish all that I wish to convey, and as I said before Philosophy is big, it contains so many mysteries.

I am not perfect and never will be, but if I at least have a goal or a source of greatness within me (as I believe everyone has greatness), I will gain a feeling of success. No one's a failure who tries, even though a person may not be successful. It's the feeling that generates inside that counts.

The first step is to believe in yourself. One who does not will always think in terms of failing. Gain a strength of "I can succeed" and have no doubts. In the quiet moments of each day, stop and meditate and repeat such thoughts as "I'm well and happy and strong" and have faith in those thoughts. True, you could meditate on the material things, but one who is interested only in the bodily comforts of life must go farther to seek happiness with himself. I once read of a man who considered himself poor because he lacked money. No one is poor who has courage and faith. The greatest example of a man mastering his physical surroundings and spiritual self was Christ. Christ had no money; he was a teacher, yet he was greater than a king. He surpassed men of all time.

Another comfort at all times is your Religion. People all over the world have many different codes of Religion. As for me, every man to his own belief with blessings. I believe it's developed in you with the aid of a church. I attend churches of many types to hear what any priest or minister has to contribute. I may not thrive on all that he says, but the thoughts that I consider worthwhile I strive to carry out in my everyday life. My Religion is deep and it would take many chapters to explain it, but basically I turn to it to get an inspiring lift and stimulation of thoughts.

Think good of all and they in turn will think well of you. If you must talk about someone, bring out the best of that person. At least give everyone the benefit of a doubt. Never preach to anyone unless they need and want your guidance. People like to talk, and a friend is one who listens. The obstinate character will seek safety when the ship is sinking.

On subjects that are discussed and brought up in a group

that you know very little of, talk slightly for you may not know the facts. If you add the wrong two cents, you will probably show your ignorance or cause a great amount of harm. People create skepticism toward subjects they know nothing of. Never disbelieve in anything until you know the score.

Avoid any sort of depression within yourself. Have will-power enough to destroy thoughts that tend to break your morale. Once you slip into a depressed mood—escape. You may become so absorbed in your so-called failure in yourself that it may take months to regain a normal life. Everyone becomes depressed at one time or another and the moment you do, work at something that draws your mind away from yourself.

At all times retain a good sense of humor. Everyone creates a liking for the optimist. The colorful side of life is relaxing.

You don't have to be up on Mrs. So-and-So's dress style, but everyone has something in common with good books and music. Everyone likes to contribute in good conversation. Just as beautiful music stirs your innermost thoughts, books place ideas into you, and conversation brings to the surface so many half-realized thoughts of your own.

It takes all kinds of people to make a world; one person is inclined to believe differently than another but each has something to contribute. Here I have tried to explain my philosophy of life. My thoughts are scattered, my language crude, but I have at least expressed some of the ideas that will be good to develop.

PART ONE

Early Years

My grandmother (Margaret Inglis) and me, 1929

The Beginning

This is the story of my journey through life to understanding what reality is.

It started with my birth on September 21, 1928, at Asbury Hospital in Minneapolis, Minnesota. My mother and dad had three children prior to my entrance into their family. My sister Carolyn was twelve years old when I was born. Dick was ten and John was eight. I was told by my sister, years later, that I was a surprise. You can expect the unexpected from me.

Shortly after my birth, my father came to the hospital waving a piece of paper proclaiming that he had just bought 200 acres of land in northern Minnesota at $2 an acre. My mother was dumbfounded. She couldn't believe he had done such a thing—and what would they do with the property? My dad replied that they could build a cabin for summer recreation for the four children they now had. Having come from Chicago, my mother was almost in shock. It just did not compute at that time. (I will return to this story later and reveal what a godsend that land eventually became. I think that the property at the present time must be worth at least $200 an acre.)

My brother John was very disappointed when he discovered that I was basically bald-headed and definitely not like the two-year-old girl next door. Somehow he did get attached to me, though, and he was a great brother.

My first remembrance of life around me was my mother rocking me and singing to me in a melodious voice. The wallpaper, which I became acquainted with at a later age, had all sorts of balloons with colorful elves floating on them.

When I was still an infant in my mother's arms, her mother came by train to see her latest (and final) grandchild. My grandmother had had eleven children, my mother being the youngest, so another grandchild was probably not a big deal to her. My mother waited in the car with me cradled in her arms, while my father went to pick up my grandmother inside the train station and brought her back to the car. I wasn't talking yet. But my mother claimed that as she was presenting me to my grandmother I leapt into my grandmother's arms and said "Mama!" My mother was totally shocked. From then on my grandmother began to favor this grandchild, and I was always cuddling up to her.

My mother had never warmed up to the idea of reincarnation, but as she pondered it she began to wonder. As I got older I looked more and more like her older sister, Jean Inglis. At the age of seven, Jean fell into a well that had bad water, and she died of typhoid fever soon afterward. This occurred several years before my mother was born. I was actually named after her, Jean Inglis Thayer. Mother had a picture of Jean in a quaint outfit of the 1880s, and next to that was a picture of me when I was older. Someone asked my mother why I was dressed up in that costume, and of course my mother explained it was her sister. I also used to use quaint sayings that were from the 1880s. Actually my mother was pretty convinced, but I will leave that up to the reader. Even stranger was that at the age of seven I became very ill with a high fever. When they took me to the doctor, he couldn't figure out what had caused it. Possibly it was an old record of the past I was reliving? Truth is stranger than fiction.

Jean Inglis, 1885

John and Margaret Inglis, 1870s

Falsely Accused

My mother, Frances Inglis Thayer, was born in Chicago in 1893. Her father, John Inglis, came from Scotland and her mother, Margaret Inglis, from England. Their families had moved to Canada, and that is where they met each other and eventually married.

My grandmother was a tiny thing, about five feet tall, but my grandfather was a big man. Apparently he was a pretty tough character when he was young. He was in a few brawls now and then, and he was footloose and fancy-free. In 1861, when the Civil War was just about to break out, my grandfather and a roughneck friend of his came down from Canada to New York. President Lincoln was calling for troops, and there were handbills all around Sackets Harbor. My grandfather and his friend decided to join the army without knowing what it was all about. They probably joined just for the fight —they liked to rough people up. They enlisted in the Ninth

New York Cavalry.

My grandfather fought almost through the whole war. He actually rose to a confidential position with the generals. He had marvelous executive ability and was fearless. Once he was assigned to carry a message to the president, which was very perilous because he had to go through Confederate lines and return. He always returned safely from his missions.

Another time he was with his friend on picket duty overlooking Warrenton, Virginia, where the Confederates were encamped. He and his friend had looked very carefully over the hill and saw no one. They retired to a rail fence and were standing there when a bullet struck the heart of his friend. My grandfather ran for cover in a wooded area, where he stumbled and fell flat. Raising himself up, he found a small book on the ground. It was a Bible that had belonged to a Confederate soldier. He picked it up and saw the words, "Saul, Saul, why persecutest thou me?" He told others that it was like a knife went through him, and from that time on he became a professed Christian.

Shortly before the war ended, my grandfather received a message from Ontario that his mother was dying. As she was a widow, an officer gave my grandfather permission to go back to Canada to help her. However, the officer failed to report the situation. The war ended, so my grandfather never returned to the army. It went down on his record that he was a deserter.

My grandfather was never exonerated by the government, and it remained on his record that he had deserted. When he was asked if that bothered him, his reply was, "No, I know in my heart what I did."

Over the years my grandfather became a crop expert. He could look at a field of wheat and tell the farmer how much it would yield. He traveled all over Europe inspecting fields, and he became well known both there and in the United States. Eventually he was hired to go to Chicago because of his talent, and he had his own column in the Chicago paper. He passed on about the time I was born.

An Unexpected Visitor

My father was also originally from Chicago. He was born in 1890. His father was an importer of china—exquisite plates and gold pieces. His company was named Thayer & Chandler. It was a very prominent business, and my grandfather was well known in Chicago.

One day when he was about 60, my grandfather was walking around in the city. Apparently he wasn't feeling well. He went into an old hotel. It wasn't the best hotel—not in a very good neighborhood. He got a room, lay down on the bed and died. That was just before I was born.

My father's family lived next door to the family of Frank Lloyd Wright (yes, *the* Frank Lloyd Wright). My father grew up with the Wright boys and was very close to Frank's son John, who was about my father's age.

A few years down the line my father and mother were married and eventually moved to Minneapolis, where my father started an investment business. When I was a new-born babe, we had an unexpected visitor come to our house. That visitor was Frank Lloyd Wright, now famous, who was on the run from the authorities.

Frank had left his wife some years before, but she wouldn't give him a divorce. They had six children and she was going to remain married to Frank, come what may. In the meantime Frank had had an affair or two. Now he had crossed state lines (from Wisconsin to Minnesota) with a woman who was not his wife. This was illegal under the Mann Act.

Frank came to our house because my dad was his friend and he needed shelter. My family graciously took them into our home—Frank, the love of his life Olgivanna, and her daughter Svetlana. Olgivanna was a very lovely, soft-spoken woman. She was originally from an area near Russia and was a Montenegrin dancer. Svetlana was my sister's age, twelve years old, and they became friends.

Frank's wife had had him trailed over the years, so the trap was set at this time. During their time at our house, Frank got restless and wanted to go to a play in downtown Minneapolis. My dad warned him that it would be foolish to attend the theater, but Frank went anyway. Frank Wright stuck out in any crowd because of his long flowing hair, stately stature, and the long cape he always wore. It didn't take long for the authorities to spot him, and the hunt was over. He was now in jail.

My dad went down to bail him out, and as he approached Frank's cell, he said, "Well, well—Frank from *Who's Who* to the hoosegow!" My dad paid the fine and took him back to the house. However, that was short-lived because it turned out that the jail had been infested with bedbugs. Soon we all moved to a hotel while they fumigated the house for the little critters, compliments of the city jail.

Frank finally was able to move to a cottage out on Christmas Lake not far from Minneapolis. He was anxious to write his autobiography. A very dear friend of ours, Maude Devine, became his secretary, and he completed his book at that time. In the book he mentioned my dad and his statement when Frank was behind bars, "from *Who's Who* to the hoosegow."

Our family home at that time was located far outside the city, south of Minneapolis, in a lovely wooded area with broadleaf trees and rolling hills. We lived on Minnehaha Parkway. Just across the road from us down a steep hill was an enchanting creek, and across the road on the far side was another steep hill. I actually remember, when I was a bit older, leaving my body at night and taking flight over those hills. However, I don't remember anything beyond that point.

The house was a square yellow stucco with a red tile roof. Frank wanted my father to let him draw up some plans that would improve the family's living quarters. My dad finally agreed to the idea of doing a makeover.

The program turned out to be quite expansive and expensive. Frank designed a large curved bay window in the living room that welcomed the sunshine in. He changed the whole format of the front door and placed a false balcony over the now-fancy mahogany door, which complemented the effect and made it classy.

But the most extraordinary room was a new one Frank built off the landing from the stairs next to the living room. Frank added a large door and extended a large room out over the back driveway with graceful arches beneath. From both the outside and the inside it looked very attractive. This same room had lovely wood paneling with large wood-latticed windows all around. The final touch was a beautiful curved fountain on the east wall that flowed all the time and was used for a fish pond. (The fish pond was still there when I dropped in on the current owners in about 1999 to tell them about the history of the house.)

In the dining area, Frank placed another small curved window with a lovely curved seat that extended to the floor, so you could sit and look comfortably out the window. Beyond the dining area he added on a room that you entered through French doors. The whole side of the house became an enclosed porch with windows all around it. The kitchen had an access door at one end that allowed the other end of the room to become a breakfast area. Also in this area was another fountain with a fish pond. In the front of the building just outside the new closed-in porch, Frank placed an outside L-shaped screened-in porch. The view was exquisite and expansive from all the windows.

My dad was astounded at the cost. But Frank never considered costs; he did his design by his genius.

A Story My Mother
Often Told

$\mathcal{M}$y mother was a great storyteller, and she loved to entertain the younger crowd with her stories. She had a way with words and descriptions. This is a special story she often told because it was so vivid we always encouraged her to tell it. It is a true story that happened to her when she was 21 years old.

My mother's sister, Helen Inglis, was a physical education teacher for a private school called Hillside, in Spring Green, Wisconsin. The school was run by Frank Lloyd Wright's two aunts, and the building, of course, was designed by Frank. He also had a very modern house not too far from the school, which he shared with his current paramour. Her name was Mamah Borthwick and she had her two children with her. She was from Europe and was separated from her husband, while Frank was still married to his first wife, who would not give him a divorce.

In August 1914, the two aunts were trying to put on an operetta for the Spring Green area and were looking for singing talent. My Aunt Helen mentioned that her sister Frances (my mother) had a very nice singing voice, and Frank's aunts encouraged my mother to come to the school to be a part of the festivities. My mother never felt she was qualified, but the aunts invited her anyway just to help out. My mother made arrangements to get train fare, and a few hours later she arrived at the Spring Green station.

My Aunt Helen met my mother at the station and told her the gruesome tale of what had just occurred, which was beyond belief. Frank was out of town, and his house had been destroyed by fire. Mamah Borthwick and her children had been brutally murdered. The suspect was a handyman Frank had hired. The local authorities were combing the area for the handyman, and up to that point he had not been found. Frank was on his way back to Spring Green.

Apparently the handyman had been unhappy with Frank about something to the point that he was enraged. Mamah and her children were sitting in one area of the house and the handyman locked all the doors and windows. He set fire to the house, and as they tried to escape he did a hatchet job on each one. It was beyond anyone's comprehension.

When my mother and her sister arrived at the aunts' home, there was chaos and total confusion. My mother was enlisted in helping them. Body parts were being brought in, and my mother actually carried covered receptacles with body parts in them.

As evening approached, everyone was exhausted. My mother was grateful to have a lovely room at the top of a winding staircase. It was a short-lived rest—there was a big commotion at the front door. My mother went to the balcony and peeped down to see a man with long hair and a flowing cape being greeted in the foyer. She immediately went back to her room. Frank ascended the stairs to seek out the room where Mamah Borthwick's body had been placed, which happened to be next to my mother's room. Soon Frank began moaning. His moaning continued throughout the night, and my mother could not sleep. At dawn Frank left the room, only to return after an hour or so.

When Frank returned, they moved the coffin down the stairway onto a horse-drawn cart. The casket was covered with flowers. Frank took the horse by the reins and walked it to the cemetery, where they placed his beloved in her final resting place.

The local authorities continued to try to track down the suspected culprit of this terrible deed. Hours later, they found the handyman. When they inspected the asbestos furnace, which had not been consumed by the fire, they discovered he had crawled into it.

Once the situation settled down, my mother became familiar with the lovely surroundings, and Frank's two aunts went back to their duties at Hillside. My mother met a young student who was about her age. Her name was Mildred Thayer.

Mildred had an older brother she wanted to introduce my mother to. About a year later at the age of 22, my mother married Cleaver Thayer. Oddly enough, they were both from Chicago but they met in Spring Green.

With my mother at the Big House

Early Life at the Big House

I grew up in the yellow house near Minneapolis that we came to call the Big House. My mother was a great mentor. She often gave me graphic lessons when she felt it was necessary. Once when I was probably five years old, I was unhappy about a lesson she was imparting to me and I told her I was going to leave. My mother told me that might be best and she would help me pack. She proceeded to get my little suitcase out and asked what I would like to take with me. Suddenly the enormity of the situation hit me, and I de-cided I did not want to go. She said she was very happy that I had made that decision. She gave me a big hug and told me how much she loved me. That made me feel very special.

As I grew up, my mother had total trust in me. Often I would go around visiting the neighbors, and they always welcomed me in. In those days we did not have the violence that is prevalent and seems to be picking up speed at this time of 2007. However, my mother always kept a watchful eye on me, except one time when I was running around on my tricycle. Harriet Avenue was just beyond our driveway, and it was pretty steep. As I was riding on our drive, I got a little venturesome. I decided to head down Harriet Avenue, which would take me down past Minnehaha Parkway. In fact, it crossed over Minnehaha Parkway and converged with another street on the other side of the bridge. I was going at top speed, and I did not realize I was going to tangle with an oncoming car. Whoever the driver was, he stopped just in time. I remember the screech of the tires and somebody standing over me to see if I was alright. I never mentioned it to my mother, but I suddenly became very wise that day.

Then there was a special lady named Mrs. Warness. Her house was located up the big hill on Harriet Avenue. She had a personality that brought many neighborhood children to her door. We appeared especially on days when she was baking cookies. She had grown sons but she loved to have the youngsters around. I probably was her biggest pest, or test. When I was very young she taught me how to make beds "properly," and I was so proud to show my mother how to make a proper bed. I would help Mrs. Warness do little things around the house, just like I would help my mother at home. Occasionally I would bother the Warness family on a Sunday at dinnertime. I was always welcomed in, but I had to sit still and listen to classical music with them until they were finished. That is when I became a lover of classical music.

Christmastime at the Warness house was special for all the children. We were invited in to help decorate. The ornaments had been accumulated over the years, and they were all different. The tree was always big, and when all the ornaments and the lights were on, it was really exciting. Mrs. Warness must have had the patience of Job to work with us very active children. I have never forgotten her. She, as well as my mother, was one of the molding factors and the nourishing of my soul in those early years. I was truly blessed.

There was something about neighborhoods in those days. It seemed that the children were always out playing and connecting with one another. We were fortunate not to have televisions or computers. We learned to be creative on our own and to think for ourselves.

In our neighborhood there was a young man about 26 years old who had Down syndrome. His name was Herbert, and he loved to watch the local kids play softball on a lot not far from our home. The boys asked him to join them one day, and he was so excited. They showed him how to hold the bat in front of him, and then the pitcher made sure the ball hit his bat. The next step was to encourage him to run the bases to home plate while they fumbled around with the ball. Herbert couldn't have been more thrilled. They made him the mascot of both teams so he could wave everybody around the bases. There is nothing like being the top dog out in the field and being loved at the same time.

The cabin in the North Woods

The Cabin Adventure

Now this is where the "godsend" started to manifest over a period of 40 years. As I mentioned earlier, my mother was in the hospital with a new baby (me) when my father told her that he had purchased 200 acres of land. The property happened to be on two lakes. The road to that area was miles of dirt road from a small post office village called Merrifield.

Dad contracted a man by the name of Bill Gibson to start working on a cabin. Bill was a typical backwoods man—tough, burly, and capable of doing the job. The cabin started out as a large square building with log siding and very attractive wood paneling for the walls. The living room was quite large, with an open loft on each side. Bill built a large rustic fireplace out of rocks indigenous to the area. After a while, a two-car garage was built out away from the cabin. A guest house was soon added, and of course, given the era, the usual two-hole outhouse beyond the guest cabin. My brothers and sister loved the cabin. I was a toddler at the time, with lots of room to grow.

Eventually Dad had a very attractive log fence built, which separated the cabin from the dirt road and its dust. As time went on, beautiful gardens were established here and there. My mother had great talent with flowers, and they were always in abundance around the cabin. Bill Gibson, the wood genius, made some hollowed half-logs on chains and placed them artistically on the log fence. These held flowers, too, and helped separate the cabin from the dusty road.

By this time I guess you have realized that my mother did adapt to the situation. After initially stating that she might spend weekends at the cabin, now it was summers—and before long it was winters, too. We had beautiful grass, beautiful flowers, and a lake we could see from our dining area with its unique round table that had extra boards to enlarge it to seat at least 20 people comfortably.

The cabin faced south, and my dad always planted Heavenly Blue morning glories that grew up on strings. When they bloomed, the living room gave off a soft blue glow. It *was* quite heavenly.

Once the roads were better cared for, our family and friends came up to build their cabins along with the Thayers. My dad sold most of the property except for 40 acres.

Maude Devine (who had been Frank Lloyd Wright's secretary) and her family had a cabin across the lake from us. Our families had a very close friendship over the years, and I called her "aunt." The Devines had a daughter named Nancy Jean, who passed on at a very early age. It broke their hearts. Soon after that, they decided to adopt a daughter. Her name was Sally, and she was about a year older than me.

I was about eight years old when we were visiting the Devine family at their cabin across the lake. It was a beautiful day, and I suggested to Sally that we take a walk through the woods. We came upon a big hornets' nest hanging from a tree limb. A few hornets were buzzing around.

I was looking at the wonder of the nest, when Sally suddenly picked up a big stick and rammed it into the hole at the base of the nest. I was so stunned and shocked that I could not speak or move. Unfortunately the hornets covered us from head to toe. It was a trauma for our bodies, and we tried to brush away the hornets as we headed for the cabin.

Aunt Maude had worked in a doctor's office and immediately saw the seriousness of the situation. We were 40 miles from the nearest town over dirt roads most of the way, and the poison could have killed us. She knew that she had to take action immediately. Thinking quickly, she grabbed a bucket and ran down to the lake, filled the bucket with mud and ran back to the cabin. She packed all our stings with the mud, which drew out the poison as it dried. We were pretty sick kids for a while, but I really do believe she saved our lives.

I never did figure out what Sally was thinking.

With my lunch box at the cabin

Journey to California

After the stock market crash in 1929, it was very difficult for my dad to continue his investment business. On top of that, his partner absconded with company funds and shortly after that committed suicide. My dad had to pay all his investors back. Basically he was wiped out. He had to rent out the Big House just to keep above water.

We moved to California in 1934. My Aunt Helen and her husband, Roy, had a dry-cleaning establishment in San Diego. Dad rented a little bungalow in La Mesa, not too far from San Diego. Carolyn, Dick and John attended high school in La Mesa. Carolyn would graduate at the end of the year and be out on her own. I was ready for first grade after kindergarten in Minneapolis.

Dad drove a van delivering dry cleaning for my Uncle Roy. As for my mother, she was always a master in the cooking arts. Probably she had learned a lot in the large family she came from. She began experimenting with making very light raised doughnuts. As soon as she succeeded she got her own little business going. Many a time I was in the kitchen after a batch was done, and I would shake the doughnuts in a bag to coat them with sugar. The business began to boom, especially after my dad started selling them on his dry-cleaning route. It soon came to pass that Cadillacs were driving up to our door to purchase those luscious doughnuts.

A few years later Mother tried to get her hand back into those terrific doughnuts, but they just were not the same quality. She concluded that it had to be the flour, which in the meantime they had started contaminating with preservatives. I agree.

School was finished and summer was fast approaching. We packed up the Packard and headed back to our cabin in the beauty of the woods and lakes. However, we ran into a sandstorm driving across the desert. The storm was so intense that we could not see out of the car windows, and my dad came to a sudden stop. It was like sand-blasting. The sand was coming through the cracks, and the fine grains of sand irritated our mouths and noses. It was a frightening situation.

My mother had the good sense to calm everyone down. At that time she was involved with Unity, which is basically made up of a lot of uplifting affirmations. She kept repeating very slowly and very positively so we all could hear, "Remember, the Infinite Power is within." It had a very soothing and calming effect.

Suddenly a car with extremely bright lights went by us, and my dad immediately seized this great opportunity and started following it. The car entered the next town with the Thayer family firmly behind it. My dad tried to catch up with the car to thank them for helping us, but the car just disappeared. Divine intervention? I leave it up to the reader. As I have said, truth is stranger than fiction.

Enjoying Bonnie Lake, 1933

Our Return to the Cabin and Safe Haven

We returned to the cabin in the summer of 1935 after our sojourn in California. The cabin was very precious to us, like a haven in heaven. Summers became a time of revival and rejuvenation.

Once the cabin was finished, Dad wanted to put in a good-sized garden spot for a variety of vegetables and all sorts of flowers. About a quarter of a mile away or less, he found a fairly level spot. He started by removing the trees and fencing in about 300 feet square. The next project was to get the rabbit inhabitants outside the fence instead of inside. I will never forget that scene. We armed ourselves with pots and utensils to bang them out of there with noise. It worked, and most of them went out the unlatched gate. A few hung in there but we finally got them all out, and the garden began to thrive after a bit of work to clean out all the brush. Good soil was already there. We all did our share of helping in the garden, and by fall my dad and mother started canning. They knew how to be frugal through the Depression.

The school year was beginning again, and we were back at the Big House. Having passed first grade I was now in second grade. However, I soon discovered that first grade in California was like kindergarten in Minnesota. At that time, California schools did not teach reading until the third grade. When I was given a book to read in second grade in Minneapolis and I couldn't read it, they took me by the hand and I went back to first grade. It was very degrading because my kindergarten friends had gone on to second grade. But once I learned how to read I began to read all kinds of books, and when my mother went to the library I had my own little card, too.

Because my father had to move around with various jobs here and there, I had the opportunity to go to a variety of schools. Each year was a different school. I always adapted. I can't say I was the best student because there was never a flow or continuity to my learning. Some schools were more accelerated than others. I *can* say it was a great learning experience to be able to engage in a variety of situations and make many new friends.

When I was in the third grade, Dad rented out the Big House again and we traveled to Green Bay, Wisconsin, for another job. That winter my mother, father, sister and I, the youngster, were traveling to Green Bay and we got caught in a snowstorm. My dad had decided to take a shorter route where the traffic was a lot less. It soon became apparent that it wasn't the right choice. The snow was heavier and the road, having been less traveled, was not easy to navigate.

As we were traveling, a snowplow came along and buried us in a mound of snow. Dad felt sure the plow man would come back, but we had a major problem. Our exhaust pipe was covered over with snow, forcing carbon monoxide fumes back into the car. Dad shut the car off. We got out with difficulty and worked to free the exhaust pipe from the snow. We really were not prepared to do a lot of digging. We all jumped in and got the job done so we could warm up the car, and then sat and waited. It was a while before the plow returned to dig us out and the road was clear for us to head for the nearest town to find lodging.

We found the town by the line of traffic waiting to get a place to stay for the night. It was still snowing, and no one wanted to venture very far. To our surprise the town was sold out, even to floor space. It was a small town, not equipped to handle this kind of an episode. As always, Mother had faith that we would find something, and we did. A farmer opened his large house to some weary travelers. Mother, Carolyn and I were the lucky ones—we got a feather bed, and I was in the middle. Dad was on the living-room floor for the night with other gentlemen.

The next day was totally awesome. The sun came up, the skies were blue, and the countryside was serene and peaceful. It was a sparkly scene, with the sun on the new-fallen snow exposing brilliant tiny specks of colors that glistened like crystal fire. The farmer and his wife fixed a breakfast fit for kings and queens. It was one of those moments you cherish all your life.

Again we returned to our beloved cabin for the summer. Gardening was the top job, and we were all in one accord.

Years later, I was on summer break from the University of Minnesota and decided to walk through the woods to a neighbor's cabin. I took the path that went around the garden and literally stumbled over a very large object, which I soon discovered was a wayward Hubbard squash. Apparently it had decided it wanted its independence from the garden, and the vine had wended its way out into this rather quiet, lonely spot. I called to my dad, who was in the garden at the time, "Come and see what I have found!" He was soon at my side and exclaimed, "My goodness!" We got the wheelbarrow and hauled it up to the cabin. It turned out to weigh about 40 pounds. I took it down to the sorority house, and we had delicious squash for days!

In my early teen years, I had two boy cousins who came north with their families in the summer. One was a year older than me and the other was about my age. With all that running room, it was idyllic. We had great, wholesome fun swimming, fishing and sailing. A lot of fun games we made up ourselves, including a lot of competitive games. There was a raft just off the shore about 30 yards from the landing dock. We would take a piece of soap that would sink, toss it into the deep water and chase it all over underwater to see who could grab it. Often when you grabbed the soap it would slip out of your hands, especially with a little shoving and pushing from someone else. You had to get the job done before you came up for air—which meant you had to have a good pair of lungs! Now, how simple can a game get, and still be a lot of fun. It was a real underwater sport.

My dad loved to sail; it was one of the hobbies he pursued most of his life. The first boat we had on little Bonnie Lake was a small sailboat that we all loved to sail in. Sometimes we would turn it over on purpose, just for a little excitement. Then we had an opportunity to purchase a boat that belonged to a fraternity brother of my dad's from Duluth. He had the boat on Lake Superior. It had a mainsail as well as a jib sail, and it was quite wide with room for more on board. We located it on the bigger lake, called Bass Lake. It could go a lot faster than the little boat and cover many areas of the lake.

One very windy day my brother John and I went over to the big lake to go sailing, which was a bit foolish. When we were out in the middle of the lake a big gust of wind caught us by surprise. It was so intense that the rudder broke to some extent. When we tried to get the mainsail down, it whipped around and got torn. We managed to get back to shore to dock the boat with just the jib sail. Of course, the next problem was to inform Dad. When we approached him with our story he didn't take it too lightly. John informed him about the mainsail being torn. That was bad enough, but when Dad found out the rudder was broken he blew up a bit.

With two cousins around for the summers we did a lot of fishing, which was quite competitive at times. We used our rods with artificial bait just to see how good our aim was in casting. We also brought fish home to be cleaned and cooked. Often I liked to go fishing by myself in the evening when it was quiet and I could watch the sun set. I was casting alone one time, and I snagged a pretty good fighter. I was a bit tensed up in getting this one aboard, but I finally succeeded. It was a good-sized bass. In those days artificial bait had two hooks, which each had three barbs. I was trying to get the hook out of him and he was trying to shake loose, and in the process I got hooked by the artificial bait, too. He was hooked with one hook and I was hooked with the other. I was trying to get him loose and now I had to get myself loose. It was a tussle, but I won. It turned out he weighed seven pounds.

In Brainerd, which was about 35 miles south of the cabin, there used to be a Paul Bunyan exhibit. The legendary Paul Bunyan was a giant lumberjack with an ox and an ax, and there was a huge statue of him. They used to have casting contests there, and when I was about thirteen or fourteen I thought I would give it a go. I was competing with some older men, and they were a bit surprised when I walked off with third place. Practice makes perfect, and I had had plenty of that.

Our cabin played host to many guests over the years. My mother always provided a meal for unexpected guests. Her leftover food never remained left over for very long. After inviting guests for a bite to eat, it wasn't long before she would have a meal on the table with all the trimmings. I think that she had a genie she conjured up, but mostly this Jeanie learned to be a small hostess for the guests.

My brothers often worked odd jobs to earn pin money, but when duck hunting season arrived, they made sure they were not involved in outside jobs. This was a big deal, and they enjoyed getting out there and building blinds on the two lakes. I was about eight years old, and I learned to be quiet if I had the opportunity to go with them. I got to row the boat when they needed to change positions on the lake if a flock of ducks happened to fly over. Believe me, I was gung-ho to go, and there were never any complaints from me. I made myself an asset to the hunt—and yes, I helped clean the birds, too.

During my years at the cabin I became good friends with the loons, the Minnesota state bird. They are aquatic birds that live totally on the water. They cannot walk on land because they have short legs. They forage for fish and most likely tasty weeds. Their sound is very melodious. They can be heard during the night and the day when flying overhead, as well as on the water. They also make a high-pitched sound when they are in distress. I learned to imitate them to a tee. Often when I was on the lake in the boat I would see loons here and there, and I would imitate their call. They would come around the boat, very curious about the stranger in the crowd.

A friend of the family came up one weekend and stayed in the guest cabin. She was aware of my "loony" call, and she complained to my mother that I was up in the middle of the night doing it. My mother laughed and told her that's what loons do at night when they fly over. It is the great sound of the North Woods.

In the thirties and forties, our phone communications at the cabin were very archaic. I am sure you have seen the old crank phone in some form or another. It hung on the wall, with the crank on the side. It was a party-line situation. We had at least 20 people on one line, each with a different ring that you cranked out for the different parties. Ours was five short rings and one long ring. You could tell who was being called because all the rings were heard up and down the system.

There were some busybodies who just loved to listen in to conversations. It was like TV addiction, and that was their entertainment. The more people got on the line, the less you could hear. Sometimes people would say, "Get off the line, folks," and you would hear a few clicks. Of course, young people had a blast, and often you would have several on the line talking.

When there was a fire in the area, they would ring five long rings. You would pick up the phone to locate the fire, and go to the spot to help out if possible. Once after hearing the location, one guy asked which way the wind was blowing. It was blowing toward the house of someone he didn't like, and he said, "Let it go." It was obvious they were not good friends.

Paratroopers

PART TWO

Wartime and Beyond

My prize poster, spring 1942

Life in the War Years

Summer was over, and we returned to the Big House in the fall of 1940. War was brewing on the horizon and the situation looked very foreboding. The citizens of the United States were well aware that war was imminent. Patriotism was very high in this country, and we were all on the same page. Both of my brothers had joined the National Guard and were being trained at Camp Ripley near the small town of Little Falls, Minnesota.

I turned 13 in September of 1941. Dick was 23 and John was 21. They both decided they did not want to be in the infantry, so they transferred to the Air Corps. We all had deep concerns about the future for Dick and John, and I was always tuned in to my little radio. I was acutely aware of what was going on around the world, like everyone else who had loved ones in the service of our country.

In the winter of 1941, we were at the Big House and I was

in seventh grade at Ramsey Junior High School. On December 7, I was listening to my little radio when the announcer interrupted the program and said that Pearl Harbor had been bombed. I ran downstairs to my family, and they had heard it, too. It was beyond our comprehension, and we couldn't have been more shocked.

Dick and John were eventually assigned to Camp Claiborne, Louisiana, and they both trained to be pilots. Dick washed out as a pilot but he did become a sergeant with the Air Corps. He was sent to India, where he and his crew flew the Hump (over the Himalayas to China). Lt. John Thayer did become a pilot, and he eventually was sent to England to fly B-17s over Germany.

When I was still in the seventh grade, there was a poster contest with a patriotic theme to encourage people to buy war stamps. Drawing was my hobby at the time, so I entered the contest. I had a theme worked out, and my mother and I went down to the dime store and bought the materials needed, including a poster board. It was quite a large poster. I drew a big sun near the top on the left side with beautiful gilt rays shining upon the western hemisphere. The rays enveloped North America and South America. In an arc at the top in bold lettering it said, "BUY DEFENSE STAMPS," and a caption at the bottom said, "May the sun never set on our freedom." I won third prize.

As usual we went north for the summer, but we never had an opportunity to go back to the Big House. My dad sold it in 1942 because the taxes were such a burden. Unfortunately, at that time houses were being sold for less than nothing. Dad took a big loss and sold it for $10,000. I am sure it would sell for at least $200,000 in today's market.

The cabin was now our permanent home. By this time it was modernized and expanded to suit our needs. When fall rolled around, we lived in an apartment in Brainerd through the spring so I could attend ninth grade at Franklin Junior High.

It was in this apartment that we received the bad news that John was missing in action. When the telegram arrived we were stunned and saddened. My mother appeared very calm and kept saying, "He will be found, he is alright." She was firm about it. My dad went into a deep depression, and it was hard on my mother as well as me. In about a month my dad decided to get employment at a defense plant in Brainerd, because he had two boys out there who needed his help. It was a saving grace. My mother's calm attitude and our firm belief that John was coming back contributed to his decision.

Spring came, and we went back to our beloved retreat in the woods. Dad commuted to work in Brainerd, and we kept the gardens going for the summer with his help on the weekends. Dad was now considering the possibility of sending me to a boarding school in Duluth, so that he and Mother could remain at the cabin during the winter months. Dad had heard about this lovely Catholic school through his fraternity friend, Dr. Huderle, who was a dentist in Duluth. (It was Dr. Huderle from whom we had bought the big sailboat.)

We made a trip to Duluth and visited the boarding school, Stanbrook Hall. The building was an extension from a four-year college, connected to it by a long hallway. In the middle of the hallway between the two buildings there was a beautiful cathedral-like edifice, the chapel. The complex was on the highest hill that overlooked Lake Superior. It was all countryside, with rolling hills and beautiful broadleaf trees and some pine. At that time there was a clear view of Lake Superior.

We finally located Sister Mary, who was the principal of the school. She had such a beautiful, pleasant face and charming manners. We concluded that I would be attending this school for my sophomore year. After we discussed the basics, Sister Mary asked me if I would be interested in attending Mass in the mornings. She knew I was not Catholic. In fact, I had immersed myself in a lot of spiritual books and had studied many teachings, including *The Life and Teaching of the Masters of the Far East* by Baird Spalding. At that age, I already had a very broad view and a spiritual sense of the many facets of religion, including the Bible with its history and the great treasures of the prophets. My father's father had been a member of the Theosophical Society. Two generations of our family had followed in his footsteps in studying the esoteric books.

I knew I was there for a special reason, and my answer was that I would be very happy to attend Mass. My dad winked at me and told Sister Mary, "If you want to make a Catholic out of her, go ahead." I was a seeker from the beginning, and I didn't want to miss any steps on planet Earth.

My first year in school, I lived in a dorm with a total of 12 students. Several students had private rooms. As I remember, there were about 30 resident students and the rest were day students from Duluth, about 200 students total. Sister Timothy was our prefect; she was in charge of our dorm and "inspector general" for our area. She was also my piano teacher. I wanted to keep up the lessons that I had started earlier at the Big House on our beautiful Steinway piano. There were practice rooms in a very private, quiet area where I would often go. There I had the freedom to be in solitude with the music.

Students were required to attend Mass three times a week, but I chose to go every day. I was so impressed by the cathedral-like atmosphere, the beautiful statues and the depictions of the stations of the cross around the walls. There was a balcony at the back of the church where the nuns sang beautiful songs with the organ. To me it was magical, and I loved it.

Because I was such a devotee of Mother Mary, I can only imagine that I was in the Catholic Church in a prior embodiment. At this point I became attached to Mother Mary, and I prayed every day for my brother John, who was still missing in action, and of course for Dick too. The nuns and the other students were aware that my brother was missing, and they also gave prayers in his behalf. I always had and still have great faith in Mother Mary, the great Saviouress.

One day one of the secretaries from the office came into my classroom and whispered to the teacher that I was needed at the main office to call my mother. I charged downstairs and immediately got my mother on the phone. She informed me that John was a prisoner in Germany. I couldn't have been more excited, and I just knew he would someday be back with us. Everybody in the school was elated.

At this time my dentist in Brainerd had put braces on my teeth. My father's fraternity friend in Duluth, Dr. Huderle, was to check on my teeth every Saturday. This was quite a luxury, because if you got any demerits you were not allowed to go to town the following weekend. I had a few demerits, especially the time I took a dare and short-sheeted Sister Timothy's bed (her room was just off our dorm area). You can imagine they were not too happy with my shenanigans. But because of my teeth, I had to go to town every weekend, demerits or no. The other kids didn't like that.

The next year I returned to Stanbrook Hall and the

eleventh grade. This time I shared a room with a postulant (one who was in training to become a nun). It became pretty obvious to me that they really were trying to change me into a Catholic. My background was quite a bit different from most of them, and I wasn't about to change. That year I became the captain of the junior class's volleyball team. We even won some games against the seniors.

By and by I started to feel the pressure to become a Catholic in very subtle ways. After all, I had proved myself a real devotee to the Divine Mother, Mary. I would meet her again in the future—she was in the wings waiting for me. I left Stanbrook Hall just after the winter season to finish out the eleventh grade in Brainerd. Just before I left, a nun for whom I had little regard, Sister Benedict, declared to me that if I left I would be a failure all my life. I just considered the source and went on my way.

My new school, Washington High, was like old home week. I knew practically everybody because I had gone to three different schools in Brainerd. My dad and mother remained at the cabin, and they rented a room for me in Brainerd with a very dear blind lady. She was very independent, and I was glad to help her out when I could.

It was at this time in Brainerd that I met a very special person named Jerry Nyberg. He was totally deaf, but he was one determined individual. He drew a lot of people to him who wanted to get acquainted with him. All his friends learned to communicate with him through sign language, and I was grateful to be one of them. We enjoyed his company and his wonderful personality.

That winter during a break we had a get-together at the cabin. There was quite a gang of us from Washington High

School, and Jerry was in the crowd. My mother and father faded into the background in their bedroom so as not to put a damper on the group. To their amazement it was pretty quiet except for the laughter, because we were all basically communicating by sign language.

John and Joan, 1946

John's Battle in Retrospect

The war was still going on. I had very little contact with my brothers. Only after their return was I to know how tough war is on the individual and about the inward scars that never go away.

John was piloting a B-17 over Bremen, Germany, when they received a direct hit. The plane was going down. John made sure everyone was out of the plane before he jumped. The last man to get out froze at the hatch and was too scared to jump. No one ever practiced jumping, so it's no wonder he froze up. John did everything humanly possible to get him to jump, but the plane was fast heading for the ground. John pushed the guy out with his foot and yelled at him to pull the rip cord, but he never did. John was burdened by the incident, but there simply was not much he could do. As he made his own jump he was fumbling with his rip cord and having a problem—it just wouldn't open. At this point he had the presence of mind to say a prayer to God and it opened. He was so close to the ground that the chute made just three swings and he hit the dirt, hard.

He buried his chute, as pilots were told to do if they ditched their aircraft. It was getting dark and he spotted a farmhouse not too far away. He headed for the light and knocked on the door. Naturally the farmer was stunned and went immediately for his shotgun. John held his arms up in a show of surrender. He couldn't speak German and the farmer couldn't speak English. John, knowing very little about the Germans, said over and over, "Call the Gestapo." The farmer was really upset and kept saying, "Nein, nein, Gestapo— Luftwaffe, Luftwaffe." He did call the Luftwaffe, who came to get their prisoner. The Gestapo was not respected by the citizens of Germany. They probably would have tortured John and killed him after any interrogation.

John was put on a train and taken many miles to an inter-rogation center. He was finally confined to a small, dark cell —no lights, no window. He couldn't see anything. He started scratching on the wall as to how many days he was in there. He did have food and water shoved under the door. At the end of a few days they took him out to be interrogated. Presently he was sitting in front of an officer who spoke per-fect English. He asked the officer how long he had been in that cell and the officer said about four days. John's calcula-tion was seven days, but of course it would seem longer. He was allowed by the rules of war to give his name, rank and serial number—no information other than that. The officer got a bit chatty with him and asked John where he was from and he said Minnesota, which isn't any military secret. The officer was very familiar with Minnesota, and they had an affable conversation. Soon John was on another train being taken to a prison camp, Stalag Luft I. This was the prison camp where pilots and their crews were held, and it was near the border of Russia.

John was imprisoned for a total of eighteen months, ending in 1945. The German guards knew that the Russians were about to take over their camp. The guards left their stations and got out just as their enemy was approaching. When the Russians reached the camp, they were on horseback and looked like Cossacks. John and a fellow prisoner were not about to stick around with these heavy-duty characters. It was loose around the camp, so they sneaked off to a nearby town, went to a house and knocked on the door. With a bit of the German language now under their belt, they communicated well enough. The family was terrified of the Russians because they were raping the women in the town. They pleaded with the two Americans to stay with them and sleep at the front door, and in return gave them food and blankets. As dawn approached, John and the guy with him got out of there as fast as they could. They were in a dangerous situation themselves if the Russians suddenly appeared. By the grace of God, they continued on until they were in friendly territory, and it became history. John was on his way home.

John's homecoming was a thrill for all. We were at the bus to meet him. We were shocked to see how thin he was. But it didn't take long with good home-cooked meals for him to start to get his muscles back, and with a little extra help from the barbells his physical appearance improved.

John began hitting all the fun spots, usually dancing and live music around the area, where he got acquainted with Joan Lindsay, whose family had a summer cabin about 30 miles north of us. To his surprise, she said she had met him when she was very young and he was about sixteen. He had had a job on a brush crew clearing out the woods near where she lived. He had come to the door needing to fill up a water jug. Even then she had thought he was cute. Now here she was an attractive young lady, and John was a good-looking young man. He knew her brothers, who had attended Washburn High, the school near our home in Minneapolis. In about a year they were married, and I was one of the bridesmaids. Joan and I have been like close sisters for all these years.

Brother Dick and His War Story

$\mathcal{D}$ick's story is not a happy one, and I would call him a war casualty that should never have happened. He served most of the war years in India. We never really knew all that he went through. When he returned to Minnesota, he was placed in a VA hospital near St. Paul. Most of his gear was stored in our garage at the cabin. One day I was looking through some of his things, and I found a Purple Heart that he had apparently been honored with.

I do know that while he was in India he became ill from a tick bite and had a very high fever. For some reason they gave him insulin, which exacerbated the situation. It seemed it was hard for him to sort out the realities from the unrealities. The war didn't help, and no veteran ever returns home the same. War is like living in hell.

Dick did not get a hero's welcome, and he had quite a lengthy stay at the VA hospital. Our family did not know what was going on. My father began checking into why he was being kept so long. He traveled to St. Paul to question the hospital personally. Dick was the one who informed Dad about the treatments he was getting. Unfortunately, they were using shock treatments on him. It was a barbaric method that they no longer use. They ended up giving him 32 treatments, and one is bad enough. This was an abuse beyond abuse—they were definitely experimenting.

Dick told my dad that he was strapped down on a table, a piece of wood was put between his teeth and a device was placed over his head by which they would send jolts of electricity to his brain. Afterward he remembered nothing until a few hours later. He was allowed to wander around unattended while in this state. Apparently there was a café not far from the hospital, and he would go there frequently to eat. One day after a shock treatment he went to the café and walked back into the kitchen and fixed his own breakfast. The people at the café had become friendly with Dick, and they just let him do what he wanted to do.

My dad got Dick released from the hospital and brought him back to the cabin, where he was able to get his feet on the ground. However, the damage was done, and he was never really the same.

In a few short months he met a girl whom he soon married. She had been a Wave during the war. They had three children, but it was not a successful marriage and ended in a divorce. The war had taken its toll, and it had played havoc with Dick's psyche. He spent the rest of his life in and out of VA hospitals. He passed on at the age of 80 in the VA hospital in St. Cloud, Minnesota.

Dick was a gentle soul and very kind to me as his kid sister.

I repeat, war is hell for those who are sent into the battle. They are scarred emotionally, physically and mentally. Dick was a war casualty that should not have happened.

High school graduation, spring 1947

Final Years of High School

In 1946, I started my senior year at Washington High School, but my dad and mother decided to go to California for the winter. My Aunt Helen and Uncle Roy invited us to stay with them again. They still lived near San Diego. That was a bit of a problem for me, because I had to take a bus to and from school and it was a good 45-minute trip. Hoover High had approximately 5,000 students; it was the only major high school in the area at that time. Here I didn't adjust to the situation too well. I went to all my classes, and it seemed to me that I never saw the same face twice, or a friendly face.

Enter my beloved Uncle Frank, my mother's brother, who was retired. He and his wife lived in a lovely small town called La Jolla. They had a charming little house very close to the ocean. Behind their house was a little studio house for guests. In less than a month Uncle Frank came to meet me at the bus stop as I was just coming home from Hoover High. He was one of my favorites, and I was so pleased to see him as I got off the bus. As were walking along, he put his arm around me and asked me if everything was alright. That did it. I was almost in tears telling him how difficult it was at Hoover High. Somehow he had known something was not right with my situation. He told me that he had a solution: he was inviting my family to come and spend the winter at his studio house in La Jolla. I couldn't have been more thrilled.

We made our move to La Jolla and settled down in the two-story studio house, which had big windows practically all the way around. From the top floor you could see the ocean, which was about three blocks away. My walk to La Jolla High School consisted of going out the back door across a little meadow, and there was the school. It was like being in paradise. As for the school, it was pure joy—lots of great classmates and a curriculum I could handle.

La Jolla High was a popular place for some of the Hollywood crowd to come to do live plays occasionally. One morning I was late for school. I was running through the hallway and almost knocked a gentleman down. To my shock, it was Gregory Peck. I apologized profusely for being so careless. His response was very gracious. Gregory Peck was a handsome man, and I had it a bit reversed—instead of him knocking me off my feet, I almost knocked him off his feet.

Life at the beach was superb, and I went there as much as I could to ride those wild waves. However, I soon learned that was dangerous, because a strong current can suddenly pull you down and out. One time I was wearing a two-piece bathing suit, and the current was so strong I lost the upper part of my suit. It's a good thing my towel was handy. You don't dare panic with the pull of the waves. You wait it out, come up for breath, head back to shore and return another time for calmer waters. Fortunately, I had received excellent training in swimming in my early years in the lakes of Minnesota.

Often I liked to take walks around this quaint town. One day I ended up in a Japanese neighborhood. It was quite a beautiful area, with vegetable gardens in practically every yard. There was a small Japanese lady walking ahead of me, carrying bundles of groceries. I caught up with her to help carry her load. She spoke only Japanese. But with a little sign language she got the message, and I shared some of the load until we got to her house. She motioned to me to follow her to her garden, and lo and behold, I had an armload of vegetables to take home. There is nothing like the universal language of love and respect that we can share with one another.

Graduation time was fast approaching, and I was missing some credits for a required subject I had to have to graduate at La Jolla High. I was soon on a train headed back to Minnesota, where I was able to graduate with the credits I had. Mother and Dad stayed a little longer and came back to the cabin at their leisure. I lived in Brainerd with my cousin John Mansfield and his family until their return. I attended the prom and I was quite a contrast, because I had a golden glow from being in the sun so much in La Jolla. The rest of my classmates had winter pale faces. I graduated and headed back to the cabin for the summer.

Through the summer I was thinking about attending the University of Minnesota. Dad had always wanted one of his kids to go on to college. I did go for about two years. What I got out of it was a radical professor and his thought processes, which I did not agree with. He was definitely brainwashing the students. In this year of 2007 there are a lot of radical professors brainwashing their students. It is a great concern to me that their mind-bent has hindered our society.

I was grateful to have the opportunity to belong to the Gamma Phi Beta sorority with some really wonderful gals. My sister-in-law, Joan, encouraged me to pledge because she was in the same sorority. So we were sisters in two ways.

I was pleased that I did have some good courses at the university. It was a part of my learning process.

PART THREE

Flying High

Ready to dive into life, 1950

Other Doors Open

My brother-in-law, Russ Christensen, was a captain for Pan Am, and he encouraged me to go with the airlines. I made some inquiries and decided to apply at another airline. After an interview I was accepted to attend stewardess training in Chicago in the O'Hare Airport area. I packed my bags and left my beautiful home in the North Woods of Minnesota. Another journey in life was just beginning.

The stewardess school was a six-week course, and there were over 50 of us. At the conclusion of our training, we were allowed to sign up for the various airports across the country. The older graduates got first choice, and I was one of the older ones. You had to put down three choices. I requested San Francisco, Los Angeles or Chicago. There was one place I was avoiding, and that was Tulsa, Oklahoma. I had been there in the thirties and it reminded me of a dust bowl. I didn't think it would suit me, even though it was some years later.

When the assignments were posted, everyone was assigned but me. My name was nowhere. When I approached the teachers they were surprised, but the only thing they could do was assign me to Tulsa. My heart sank, but there was not much anyone could do to change it. Would you call that destiny, or what?

I had never flown on a plane before I flew out of Chicago, but I took to it like a duck to water. Five of us were assigned to Tulsa. We all got on the same plane on standby, which meant we could be bumped at any time. We made it as far as St. Louis, Missouri. Then all five of us got bumped, since we were nonrevenue. That meant we couldn't get out until the next day.

My brother John had moved to Alton, Illinois, not far from St. Louis. He was an investment broker and was living there with his wife and two children at that time. John came to our rescue, and we all piled into his car and crossed the river to Alton. They had a sweet little home with an upstairs and a downstairs. There wasn't enough room for all of us, so John and I slept next door at the neighbor's house. The next morning, John took us back over to the airport to catch flights for Tulsa. Everyone made it but me. I stayed behind and went back for a longer visit with the family. I wasn't too anxious to get to Tulsa anyway. John drove me over to the airport the next morning, and I managed to get on an early flight.

As we approached the Tulsa airport I was very surprised to see a sprawling, modern city. I could see that I was going to like this dust-bowl town after all. I connected with my fellow stewardesses, and they came to get me. They had already found a house that would fit us all. It was pretty far out in the country. I couldn't have been more pleased.

My first flight out was to New York City. In those days the planes had propellers and the flights took much longer. Ours was a DC-6, which carried 54 passengers and a crew of five: captain, copilot, flight engineer and two stewardesses. Part of the trip was very successful, but the other half was a great learning experience.

My cohort stewardess was not my cup of tea. I found out that life was in the fast lane for her. We arrived at our destination, the hotel in downtown New York where the crews were housed for overnights. She had an older "gentleman friend" she wanted me to meet. According to her, this kindly older man would love to take me out to a fancy restaurant for the evening. I'm no dumbhead and I was a bit dubious, but she convinced me enough that I agreed.

Yes, he did take me to the fancy Stork Club, and the meal and the entertainment were great. At the end of the event we were driving back by taxi and the conversation got to be more than I bargained for. When we arrived at the hotel, I bolted out of the car, dashed to the elevator and arrived at my room safe and sound. My fellow stewardess did not show up for the night or the next morning. I met her at the airport ready to board our return flight. Believe you me, I let her have it with both barrels. The next day I contacted the crew chief who set up the schedules and told him to never put me with that stewardess again. And he didn't.

Destiny rides again, for my next flight out of Tulsa was to San Francisco. This time the crew lineup was different. The flight was the continuing trip from New York now going to the West Coast, and it left at 2 a.m.

It was the policy that if you did not know the captain you were to introduce yourself to him, and I proceeded to do so. After the introduction I was totally caught by surprise when he said, "You're going out with me tonight?" When I said yes, he grabbed me by the arm, took me to the door and said, "Look at that beautiful full moon!" with a wolfish grin on his face. That did it. I was beginning to wonder if I was in the right line of work.

We boarded the plane and our first stop was Oklahoma City, which is a very short distance from Tulsa. After leaving the Oklahoma City airport we would fly through the night, and we would arrive at San Francisco in the morning. In the interim period, my cohort stewardess kept asking if I would take the coffee up to the crew. I told her she could do it if she didn't mind. She asked me several times, and I had the same answer. Finally she told me that Captain Allison wanted to talk to me.

At this point I had to obey the captain's orders, and I went up with my guard at full attention. Surprisingly enough, it was a casual conversation, with "Where are you from?" for starters. I told him that I was from a cabin in the woods in Minnesota. That seemed to catch his interest. At this point, he was behaving more like a gentleman. The subject got around to hunting, which I was familiar with, and he seemed totally surprised. I mentioned that I had a .20-gauge for grouse hunting and a .22 rifle for getting rid of the red squirrels that were bothering our big bluebird house. His curiosity was piqued by this time.

He started telling me about his hunting activities, from hunting big game to quail hunting, and said that he was a gunsmith by hobby. He asked if I liked to fish and graciously got around to inviting me over to meet his mother, who loved to go fishing. By this time *my* curiosity was piqued, and I said yes. He also mentioned that the quail season would be coming up soon and to have my father send me my shotgun. He explained to me that quail hunting is not like hunting grouse, which are bigger and fly more slowly. Quail fly in coveys, and he had bird dogs that scope them out. When you flush them out they rise in a frenzy, and it is unnerving at first to get a shot off. The idea is to pick out one bird and go for it. He then asked me to join him for breakfast the next morning, and I accepted.

The next day we had breakfast in the dining room of the hotel where the crews stayed. After that he wanted to show me some of the sights of San Francisco, since it was my first trip there. The next morning the crew boarded the limousine that would take us to the airport for our return flight. The cockpit was no longer off limits. Providence has its day.

When we arrived at our destination, we handed over the passenger log to the next stewardesses for the trip now headed for New York. Wayne was inside the flight crew area waiting for me to disembark, to ask if he could take me home. At that time we made arrangements for me to go on a fishing trip with him and his mother.

Wayne was divorced and had two children. Wayne Jr. was ten years old and Kathy was five years old. Wayne was seventeen years older than I. He was tall and handsome, and what made him so trim was that he was a hard worker and kept a farm running just outside of Claremore, Oklahoma. He had hired help to take care of the basics for the day-to-day upkeep of the farm. When the divorce was completed, he handed the farm over to his ex-wife with the stipulation that she would not sell it but use it for receiving income from the produce and to provide a place for his children. He would continue to work on the farm. So the farm was deeded over to his ex-wife. The agreement was short-lived, and she sold the farm at a loss. Wayne had no recourse to salvage his hard-earned investment.

Graduating stewardess, June 1951

# Changes on the Horizon

We had five stewardesses living in a bungalow way out in the country. One gal got married, and we were down to four. So we went house-hunting to find something closer and possibly cheaper, and we did. It was a two-story house on a hill in a very nice district not too far from the airport. There was a second apartment below the main part of the house, which was also for rent. I suddenly realized that my dad and mother would be going someplace south for the winter, as they had been doing for a few years. I called them immediately and informed them about the apartment below us. They were delighted and made plans to rent it. Soon they were on their way.

It was a perfect situation for all, including my dad. We no longer needed limousine service, since my dad was the official chauffeur. He would take us out to each of our flights and come and pick us up. He loved the fact that he was so useful, especially escorting these young gals around. Now and then my mother used her cooking skills to make us special dishes. We never had it so good as that winter.

There were some very interesting people on some of my flights. Flights out of Washington had some key senators on board. James Stewart and his wife were on one flight. They were very kind and thoughtful people. Milton Berle was a big hit in those days. He was a very talkative and active man. He insisted we two stewardesses have our picture taken with him. He asked the person who took the photos to send them to us, but we never got them. My all-time favorite was Bob Hope. He rang for a stewardess, and I answered the call. He was concerned for a passenger seated across and down the aisle from him who apparently was having a problem. I considered that a kind gesture. I was hoping to thank him as he departed from the plane. However, he knocked on the cockpit door and went down the unloading ramp.

As an employee of the airline, I was allowed unlimited mileage for trips. I also was able to give my dad and mother a certain amount of mileage, which they occasionally used. They made a trip to California and I met them out there. They had never been to New York, and as I was flying to New York at the time we met again there.

My dad enjoyed hobnobbing with people, and he was always friendly and talkative. As the saying goes, he never met a stranger. That reminds me of an incident in New York at the hotel we were staying in. Apparently some woman approached him in the lobby, looking for a pickup. My dad was a bit shocked, and he told us the story. It was too good an opportunity for a prankster like me to pass up. I told my mother I was going to call Dad from my room and disguise my voice and not to be too surprised. The phone rang and my dad picked up the phone and carried on a conversation with this strange woman (me) about the incident in the lobby. My dad was totally flustered, and I broke out laughing. My mother started laughing, and Dad saw the humorous side, too.

The Korean War was on at this time, and the airline made an agreement to help the troops out from time to time. Once a DC-4 landed in Tulsa, loaded with GI Joes. They needed a stewardess to take the flight on to Boston. I was the only stewardess, and all I had to hand out was coffee and doughnuts. The plane didn't have much of a galley because it was for hauling troops. However, I had no problem, and they were all eager to help me. Some of them helped pass out the goodies, and I enjoyed hearing about their experiences. By the time we landed at the Boston airport, I had all kinds of trinkets they wanted me to have. I insisted that they be sure the girlfriends did not get neglected. That was a great trip, and I hardly did anything except listen to their stories.

With Wayne

A Price on Wayne's Head

$\mathcal{W}$ayne had been an excellent pilot through fifteen years of commendable service. I was told by the other pilots that they considered Wayne one of the best. They elected him as their representative in the ALPA, the Air Line Pilots Association, formed by all the airlines. At that time, the president of the ALPA was Dave Behncke. He would help the pilots in litigation against any airline that was not fair and balanced. Wayne also saved many a pilot his job if a company proved to be unfair. He uncovered some unlawful practices and held the companies' feet to the fire through the ALPA.

Wayne knew there was a price on his head. There was an agent from the Phoenix airport whom Wayne had helped years before, back in Boston when his wife got sick. Wayne had lent him some money and allowed him to pay it back as he could without interest. But Wayne got the interest back when the agent informed Wayne that the company had placed a price on Wayne's head. Wayne told him that he knew it and thanked him for his concern. That was why as a pilot he was extremely cautious in following all the rules.

Two months after I met Wayne, in the first part of September 1951, he was removed from his job by the chief pilot, the overseer for the pilots at the Tulsa base. Wayne had had to divert his flight to the nearest airport because of a failed engine. He had followed all procedures to a tee. There was to be an inquiry about this flight. To make any charges stick, the chief pilot personally falsified Wayne's report of the incident, scratching out details to make it look like Wayne had not made the right judgment. At this point Wayne was no longer allowed to fly for the airline. I am sure that the chief pilot had no qualms about what he had done, since it was highly encouraged from the top.

The inquiry took over a year. Through several months they held long-drawn-out hearings that were exceedingly difficult for Wayne. Wayne eventually had to sue the airline for defamation of character. Dave Behncke would have been on Wayne's side, but he had been voted out of office. The new ALPA president was not cut out of the same cloth and favored the side of the company. He did everything he could to block Wayne from any assistance from the union. The pilots who voted Dave Behncke out realized later they had lost a jewel.

Many of the pilots came by Wayne's house to encourage him and backed him 100 percent. The fact that they were sticking by him gave him the courage to make it through this trying time. It never came to pass for him to come back as a pilot. (But one door shuts and another one opens.)

The cover-up was so apparent that many of the pilots

who attended the proceedings were disgusted with the airline. Wayne's case against the airline ended up in the Oklahoma Supreme Court, and the judge threw it out as having no merit. We were informed some time later by a reliable source that the judge was paid off. It should have been a win-win situation, but the trap was set and worked on from behind the scenes.

The chief pilot got away with it. His secretary saw them falsify the records about Wayne's last flight, and she took the witness stand in Wayne's defense. She got the ax big-time. She was fired and was never able to get a job in Oklahoma again. She had to sell her house and leave the state to find work—for speaking the truth.

This story was so intriguing and the conspiracy so obvious that Wayne later wrote a book about the whole event, called *Men Who Fly*. Wayne had a flair for writing. When he was a test pilot for Northrop Aircraft Company, he had written some stories for Hollywood. *Men Who Fly* had to be written. Not only was it a catharsis for Wayne, but it showed what deceptions can take place at all levels by those who are supposed to be leaders.

The case destroyed Wayne's ability to get a job as a pilot. A big oil company was about to hire him to fly their small business plane. The airline got in touch with the oil company and threatened that they would no longer do business with them if they hired Wayne. The airline was one of the biggest accounts the oil company had, and the oil company's hands were tied. They apologized to Wayne, who totally understood.

From that time on I was with Wayne between flights. I hoped I could give him a feeling of being positive about the situation. We did have a wonderful relationship, and it was obvious that I was sent there for that reason. It was a crushing blow for Wayne to be taken from flying, which was the love of his life. If I helped ease that blow in some small way, I will always be most grateful.

Flashback: Wayne's Stories

*W*ayne was an extremely fine pilot, and during the Second World War he had been one of the many chosen to fly what they called ATC (Air Transport Command). He was on loan from the airline. The ATC pilots flew big wigs and many wounded soldiers back to the States, also cargo and sometimes entertainers. They had no protection except their knowledge to keep them out of danger, which wasn't always easy.

Wayne had some fantastic stories to tell, and I hope I can do justice to a few. Once he was headed for a South American airport. He had a new copilot who was quite young and didn't have much of a clue about the war. The copilot relieved Wayne for a brief nap in his seat. Wayne had a cap pulled over his eyes, when suddenly the copilot was waking him up to show him some fireworks. Wayne was somewhat groggy, and he saw bursts of shells very close to their aircraft. He grabbed the controls and said, "[Censored]—that's not fire-works, that's anti-aircraft shells! Remind me to trade you off." Wayne immediately went to a higher altitude to get out of range and landed safely in South America.

As the story goes, later that night Wayne was playing poker with a group of pilots. When a captain he was playing with lost the bet, Wayne kept his word and traded his copilot off for the loser's copilot.

The story that sticks out in my memory most clearly is the time Wayne was flying out of Europe, headed for the Azores Islands 900 miles off the coast of Portugal. They are very small islands and somewhat tricky to land on. Some pilots miss the first pass and try again. Wayne was headed for the Azores and the copilot was checking on the tires, which were drawn up into the belly of the plane. He had his flashlight on and suddenly there was a pair of eyes staring up at him. It was a young kid. The copilot told the young man to come out of there and brought him up to the cockpit. Wayne could see that the kid was scared to death, and he was very gentle with him. The young man explained that he wanted to go back home, and that made him a deserter. Wayne told him that he had to call in and report that he was aboard.

He contacted ground control at the airport where he was landing and reported to the radio man that there was a deserter on board and that someone should be there to take charge. As they came in for a landing Wayne noticed that there were all kinds of vehicles and armored cars on the ground, which piqued his curiosity. As he came to a stop, armored cars swarmed around the plane. When they opened the door there were military all over the place ready to take over the plane. Wayne was aghast at the situation and could not believe this was for one little deserter. Ground control had passed on the word "deserters," plural. They told Wayne later that if he had missed the landing they were prepared to shoot the plane down.

As a young man Wayne won his wings through the Air Corps when it was practically in its infancy. He had been a test pilot for Northrop, and he had great knowledge of the working parts of an airplane. He also had an uncanny sense about weather and how to keep his plane and its passengers out of harm's way.

One time a dramatic weather pattern evolved. In those days you did not fly over it; you basically just did your best to avert the worst. The weather was so severe that Wayne knew he had to avoid it by climbing over it, which was unprecedented. He went to 29,000 feet, and he kept the pressure in the cabin for the passengers at 10,000 feet. He knew his plane, and with a few adjustments to the pressure system the passengers had a safe flight.

The big test for pilots was to be alert, to observe the weather conditions and to plot their flight plan wisely according to the weather patterns. I was always fortunate to be with pilots who knew their stuff. Believe me, some did not.

One of the captains on another flight was in a seemingly clear area and unwisely did not put the seatbelt sign on. He lacked either experience or good judgment. Suddenly he was in an all-encompassing storm. Many passengers were hurled from their seats. One of the stewardesses hit the ceiling, came down on a seat and severely hurt her back. On their radio, Wayne's crew heard the anguished pilots calling for an emergency landing. Apparently Wayne had warned the captain about the turbulence they might experience. Of course (as an aside), this man was a straight yes man for the airline, and the incident was never investigated nor did he get a reprimand.

Colorado honeymoon, 1952

Sequence of New Events

In October of 1952, Wayne got itchy feet to go big-game hunting, and he felt in need of a break. One day he was telling me about his various hunts in Colorado with an old-time rancher friend named Ed. He asked me to join him, and I looked at him like he was nuts. He had a twinkle in his eye and a smile on his face, and he said he would like to make it legal.

I hardly needed to remind him that in those early days of flying, there was a policy that no stewardess was to be married. Wayne's response was that no one had to know, and we would go to New Mexico, just across the border, to find a justice of the peace. I accepted but I had qualms about my family in Minnesota. I called my dad and he wanted me so desperately to come up there for the wedding. I told him that my time was limited and this would be the best way to do it. In just a few days I made plans with the airline to take about two weeks off for a little trip.

Soon Wayne and I were on our way. Our first stop was Clayton, New Mexico, where we were married by a justice of the peace. The next day we arrived at the ranch in the high plateaus of Colorado, where Ed welcomed us with open arms. He had a small rough old guest cabin that he graciously offered us. Some rough-and-tumble characters worked with him (it was a good thing I had brothers), but Ed was the head honcho.

The next day they saddled up two horses for us, and we headed for the higher range of mountains. I was not familiar with horses except for petting them, and I had some learning to do. Hunting was my cup of tea, but I had never experienced a big game hunt or especially climbing up and down the mountains. I was a flatlander from Minnesota.

After we tied up the horses there was a lot of climbing ahead, and I balked at attempting to climb a steep mountain. Wayne said, "Well, if you want to stay here until I come back, I can pick you up later." Good psychology. I climbed the mountain. From then on I was all over those mountains. They were so clear and so beautiful. After my first taste of hunting in Colorado I was hooked. The excitement is high, and it keeps you alert for the game.

We were on top of a high area looking into the valley below when Wayne spotted a herd of deer. He picked one out to shoot, and he got it. The problem was that he had to go into the valley on horseback to dress it and pack it out. He told me that it would take some time to do and suggested that I go back to the camp. My answer was "Are you crazy?— I don't know the trail." He convinced me that all I had to do was let the horse take me back. He assured me that the horse would go straight for the feed. "He knows the barn where the feed trough is."

Well, Wayne did tell me the truth, but not all of it. Yes, the horse definitely knew the way back. I thought I could guide him somewhat on a trail that would be a gradual descent. As Wayne said, the horse went straight for the feed. But since he knew he had a greenhorn on his back, he was in command. We went straight down at the fastest speed he could go, with me trying to rein him in. I hung on for dear life, and the thought of getting dumped out in the wilderness made me hang on all the more. It seemed like an eternity but he did get to the feed trough, and I jumped off in a limp state. When I told Wayne my story he was quite entertained by it, and after a while I was able to see the humorous side of the episode myself.

A few years later I had my own horse, as did Wayne. My horse had very long legs, and we called him Daddy Longlegs. He was so tall I had to have a boost to get up into the saddle. This time I was in command of the riding situation. He was a very gentle horse, and that helped.

Wayne had three dogs we always used to take when we went hunting for birds. He loved English setters and used to breed them. They were beautiful dogs, with long white fur. When we took them hunting, all three of them would go with Wayne and not with me. Wayne told me that if I wanted my own dog, I'd have to keep a puppy and raise it myself. So I did. I named him Bo. He had a very charming face with dabs of black, and his ears were brown and black. I trained him myself and he knew my commands. When we went quail hunting, he'd point when he found a covey, until I signaled him to flush out the birds. Then all hell would break loose.

Eventually I had to leave Bo behind, but that's how life is sometimes. I still have my Bo-dog's picture on my dresser. It's a sweet little picture of him on a point.

Back in Tulsa again I had to make other housing arrangements. I found a single apartment that would suit my needs. Most of my time off was now in Claremore, where Wayne and I shared the house with his mother, Mimma. I would stay at the apartment the night before my flights out, and I had Wayne's car to go back and forth.

At one time the chief stewardess at Tulsa called me into her office to question me about the possibility of my having married. Many times she would get on the flights to check out the stewardesses. She always liked me and gave me heads-up reports. She knew I enjoyed the passengers and made sure that everyone was well taken care of. Wayne had taught me how to kid with the truth, which I managed to pull off when she asked me if I was married. I laughed and said, "Of course, and I have two kids at home under the bed!" She may have figured it out, but I didn't say yes or no.

Close Calls

I remained with the airline about five years. During those years I experienced some close calls that were a bit hair-raising. The stewardess's job was to at least *appear* calm through any emergency. People were catching on to flying more and more. But some passengers were a bit uncomfortable, and you did not want to add to their stress by looking stressed yourself. Trips were a little rougher then, because they couldn't fly at high altitudes in those early days. They couldn't fly over weather like jets do now. Some pilots were not as smart as others in avoiding the bumps of turbulence.

The DC-6 carried 54 passengers. At the back of the airplane there were lounge seats for about eight people. The flights were a lot longer then, and full meals were served during flight time. We had plenty of opportunity to chat with people, which many liked to do. We were able to give them extra service since we had lots of time in the air. Often we would entertain the children and give them little jobs to do so their parents could get a break. Many a cup of coffee went up to the cockpit for the two pilots and the flight engineer.

One time I had to shift over to cover a Convair flight to Chicago and back. It had a crew with a captain, copilot and one stewardess, and it carried 40 passengers. We were in bad weather and holding our flight pattern in sequence with other flights and at different altitudes. One by one we came in for a landing. As we were holding at the altitude assigned to our flight, I entered the cockpit to bring coffee to the crew. I was just about to leave when suddenly we all witnessed a Piper Cub crossing our bow. We were within a hair's breadth of hitting his slipstream. It could have been a midair collision. The cockpit almost turned blue with anger at the control tower. They answered back and said there was no such plane scheduled in that area. The pilot was roaming around on his own, oblivious to the danger he was causing.

In an incident on another Convair flight returning to Tulsa from El Paso, we made a stop at a small town in the middle of Texas. The Convair had two engines. As we were taking off, I was immediately aware that the windows on the left side of the craft were covered with oil. I put on my high-speed effort to get the message to the pilots. They were not aware of what was happening because it was so sudden. They circled back to make a forced landing, as they called the control tower to clear the runway. With the oil in such abundance, the captain was totally amazed the plane didn't catch fire. The plane was grounded, and they had to make arrangements for the passengers to board another plane. The crew remained there for the night. We caught a flight the next day and deadheaded back to Tulsa.

It seemed to me that I was always protected. The last incident that occurred was on my final trip. I had already handed in my resignation. They removed me from my final trip to Los Angeles with my regular crew. I was disappointed when they called and wanted me to take a Convair trip on a "puddle jumper" to Chicago. I was preparing myself the night before to be ready to get out to the airport early in the morning when the phone rang. It was the field telling me that a new stewardess had arrived, and she would be taking the flight out to Chicago the next morning. I would be going with my crew that same day to Los Angeles after all.

We were in midair when the crew got the news that the Convair I was to be on had crashed. Not many passengers survived. The copilot lived but was badly hurt. All who survived had serious injuries. We were all shocked about the news—especially me, who by the grace of God missed that flight.

It took time to ferret out the cause of the Convair crash, but it soon was divulged that the airline was in big trouble. The maintenance log showed that the plane was to have gone to maintenance for repair of a cracked cylinder. There must have been some pretty sloppy communication for them to allow that plane to go out without repairs. It was called negligence. The airline was wide-open to be sued.

Some pretty shrewd lawyers were hired to get the first settlement for a passenger who had lost the use of her legs and could only move around by wheelchair. It didn't take long for them to seek out Wayne to be their adviser, since he had already been a hound dog on some of the airline's neglect. Wayne was no longer flying, but he dedicated himself to assist them. They hired me to sit in on the meetings from time to time. The airline was not aware that Wayne had been hired as an adviser. He still had his own case to deal with.

The copilot was a key to the case. He had been flown to Miami where his family was, and he was recovering in a hospital there. The law firm sent Wayne and me to Miami to have a chat with him, to see if he had some knowledge or information that might help. We discovered that he had suffered a lot of trauma to the head that caused his memory to be blocked regarding the crash. In a way it was a blessing for him, but it didn't help the case any. The trial proved gross negligence, and the wheelchair victim got quite a settlement. That settled all the cases involved, and the airline owed plenty by the time it was over.

PART FOUR

Adventuring

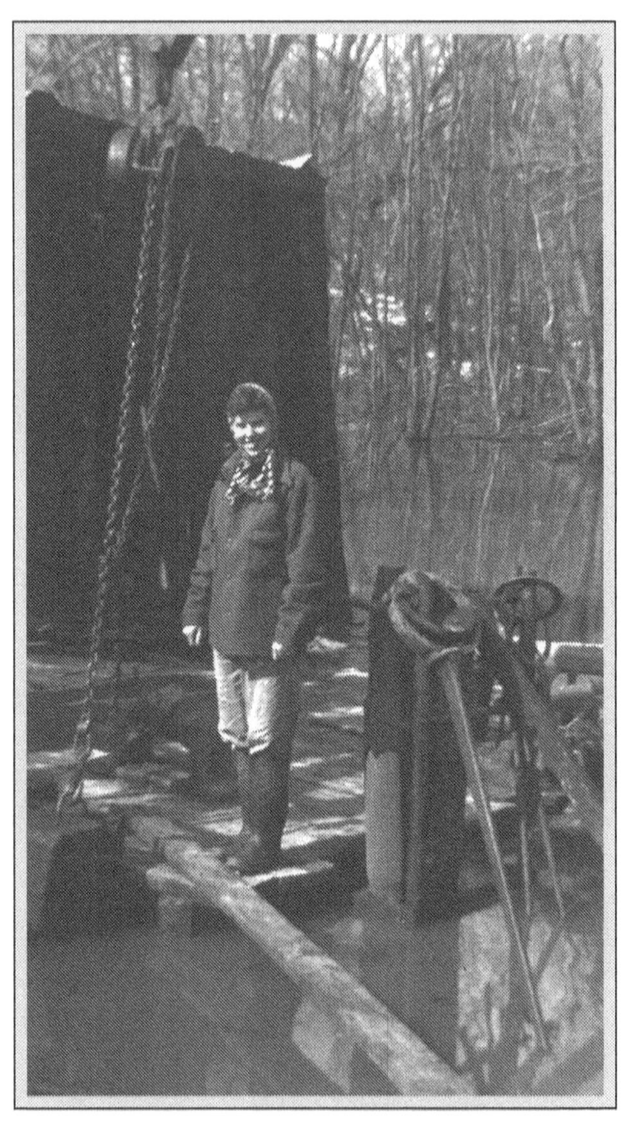

On our original oil rig, ca. 1957

Oklahoma Oil Fields

As a young man Wayne had worked with his dad, who was a wildcat oil driller and had his own outfit. Wayne's dad had always been able to supply an income for his family through the years with a few wells here and there. He passed away a few years before I showed up.

In late 1951, Wayne's case with the airline was dragging on, and he had to do something to help support his children. He was living with his mother, who had kept the house and her garden going through the years. In the backyard there was an old cable tool drilling machine stashed away that his father had used. Wayne was an old hand at the business, and as he grew up he had learned all the hard work that it takes to run a machine. He told his mother he was going to check on the old machine to see if it would be worthy to work with. When he got back to the house he called Russ, the old-timer who had worked with his dad. When he told Russ that he might get the old machine working again, Russ sounded just as eager as Wayne. They got their heads together, and soon with a few repairs it was up and running. They moved the rig out to the area his father had leased. His mother still had the lease because his dad had some small oil wells there that were still paying off under her name. Over the years Wayne had been checking the leased area to make sure the pumps were still working properly.

Both Wayne and Russ were getting conditioned again for this work, which was not easy. It was definitely not easy for Wayne to get back into that high-energy job after being tied to an airplane for fifteen years. They firmed up some other leases around the area for future prospects. It would be a while before payback time.

After I quit my job with the airline, I found a job with a doctor friend of Wayne's in Claremore. He trained me to keep the books and to assist him in minor operations. I gained a real joy in that capacity and decided that somewhere down the line I would like to pursue a course in practical nursing.

Job changes came rapidly. Wayne now had backers for the exploration of oil in a much-expanded area. You never know what the prospects will be until you start digging. Since the weather was nice, we decided that I would assist him as much as I could.

It was fortunate that I was able to work with Wayne closely. Not only was I helping to support him on the rig, but I also ran important errands when extra parts were needed out of Oklahoma City. One day a part was needed ASAP, and I headed for the big city in high gear. We had a fairly new Chrysler. I nosed it straight down the two-lane highway and made pretty good time. Coming back I left somewhat late, so I was putting the pedal to the metal a bit. I had to stop at

Claremore to pick up the mail, and as I slowed to a stop at the post office the whole front end of the car collapsed. To say the least, it was a bit of a shock. I called the Chrysler dealer. He came immediately to the scene, and even he couldn't believe it. The car sits on what they call an A-frame, and the whole front of the A-frame gave way to gravity.

I finally got the part to Wayne, and he could hardly believe the episode that had occurred. Yes, I definitely think I have a great guardian angel who just hasn't given up yet.

Once we made a trip to the city together to check on some oil leases at the capitol building. It was a long day, and we decided to spend the night at a nearby motel. We signed up for the room and then promptly went out to eat. When we returned, the clerk at the desk advised Wayne that his wife was trying to track him down and he thought he should warn him. Wayne looked him straight in the eye and said, "May I introduce you to my wife." Yes, there was a difference in our ages, and the guy was trying to pull a fast one since he already had our money. On some check-ins, that might have worked.

While I waited for my next job to appear, I kept on helping Wayne. We worked shifts during the summer months, since there was more daylight. Wayne and I got to work about 7 a.m. and worked through 3 p.m. Wayne Jr., who was a pretty good-sized kid, worked with Russ from 3 p.m. until 10 p.m. My job was to get the necessary tools to hand to the driller and to keep all the tools in their place. Wayne was the driller, and his job was to keep the cable tools moving downward into Mother Earth inch by inch.

The bits were of heavy steel about four feet tall and from twelve inches to six inches in diameter. You start with the bigger size and reduce as you go deeper. The bit gradually grinds away, and water is added to free the soil. The cuttings have to be removed according to the feel of the driller. The tool that pulls out the cuttings is called a bailer. It always fits the size of the hole and is quite long. It was my job to untie the bailer and pass it to Wayne to pick up the cuttings. Once they are picked up, the cuttings are dumped into a slush pit built into the ground next to the platform. At this point you always catch a sample. You take the samples home at night and examine them under a microscope, to see what formation you are in. You keep a detailed log, and you save and tag the sample. To see if there is any oil in the formation, you check it with a special violet light and the oil glistens like gold. Thus the phrase "black gold."

You can imagine that the drill bit is going to get flattened and also shrink in size with all that pounding, and it does. The driller is very sensitive to what is going on at the end of that line. As soon as the cuttings are dumped, the bit is checked for size. When it is at that stage, it is put into the forge until it gets red-hot. Another bit is waiting on the sidelines to replace the bit that is now in the forge. In the meantime, drilling continues until the bit in the forge is hot enough to work with. At that point all drilling stops. You place the hot bit on an iron, pound it back to its right size and give it a good cutting edge on the bottom. Usually it takes two men to do this work, but we were in the low-income bracket at the time. I had the will but not the way. It was all up to Wayne.

I actually could move large pieces of equipment because they were attached to balanced weights. It was so easy to do that I could move them practically with one finger. One humorous incident occurred when a salesman came by to chat, which they often did trying to sell something. He was surprised to see this woman dressed in men's garb and boots.

When I started to move some heavy equipment, he came up on the floor to help, and he was not dressed for the job. I stopped him in time before he got messed up and explained to him about the weights.

Life on the oil rig was interesting, especially when we had a few paying wells. The biggest well we ever got was a huge gas well that we tapped into. When the bit hit that formation it was obvious it was gas, and Wayne knew he had to pull the bit out as quickly as possible. With all that pressure it blew itself out, and soon there were rocks and gravel coming out in a big blast that wouldn't relent. From then on the ride got wilder. The well had to be capped, and at the time no one was prepared to do it. In the meantime a rock hit a light bulb, and that was all it took to burn the drilling rig down to the ground.

Wayne had to get experts to use dynamite to stop the flow of gas. It was a few days later that we got the well capped, and it was not a simple job. In Oklahoma at that time, the state wasn't interested in buying or using the gas. They apparently had an ample supply. With backers behind us now, we were able to buy a better rig that outclassed the old one by quite a bit.

Those sacks of samples we so carefully collected from each and every well we drilled began piling up in the garage. It was time to start getting rid of them. Because the samples were such rich soil, we decided to put them on Wayne's mother's garden to fertilize it before she started her planting. Mimma was the talk of the town when the vegetables starting producing and ripening. They were almost three times their normal size. It gives one reason to reflect on the fact that our soil is depleted. You wonder what is in chemical fertilizers to destroy the soil's natural fertility.

It was while we were living with Mimma that I became aware of a gas odor that was very disturbing to me. I mentioned it to Wayne. It didn't seem to affect him, probably because of the heavy odors from the wells. His mother was aware of it too, and I kept complaining. We had guests for dinner one night, and they mentioned it as soon as they entered the house. I called the gas company and complained about it. I knew it was getting to me. They came out the next day and roamed around the house. On the back porch were Wayne's clothes waiting to be washed. Because of the grime and dirt they had to be washed separately. The gas company attributed the odor to the oily clothes on the back porch. They left firmly convinced they had found the problem, when I knew they had not.

About this time Wayne started complaining, too. I called up the gas company again and told them that we were getting nauseated from the fumes. When they came out with some more equipment, they discovered that the front yard was 100 percent explosive. There was a broken gas line that ran underground on one of the main streets just a few yards from the house. The gas came through the line connected to the house, and it was devastating to say the least. The gas company was extremely apologetic and grateful to locate the line that was causing the problem. You could say we were grateful, too. Angels at work again, I really believe.

A Break in Our
Daily Occupation

In the summer of 1957, Wayne and I decided to spend some time at the Thayer cabin in Minnesota. It was our first opportunity to break away from work, and it was Wayne's first trip there.

Like many of our neighbors, Dad had had a major problem for years with skunks under the guest cabin. I had been well aware of the problem even before I left home. The skunks would dig their way underneath the cabin and take over. Occasionally they would fight, and the ensuing spray caused quite a problem for the guests. While we were there, my dad went through all the details of who had tried to help, what they had done, and how nothing ever solved the problem. Wayne said, "Cleaver, I think I can solve the problem for you." My dad replied, "Better men than you have tried"—because, of course, in his estimation, they were experts. But Wayne was a country kid. He graciously said, "Let me give it a try."

My nephews, who lived close by, and the neighborhood kids seemed to take a liking to "Uncle Wayne," who made things interesting for them. He told the children that they could help him make a box trap for the skunks. They were thrilled, and of course he made a point of having the kids fetch odds and ends for him. As he was building the trap he explained to them that skunks like to crawl into logs, so he was making a log-like trap. It ended up being about three and a half feet in length, and wide enough for the little critter to crawl into.

Now the big assignment was to find "Aunt Frances" (my mother) to see if she had any chicken or meat scraps they could use for bait, and of course she did. The children brought the scraps to Wayne, and he placed them at the very end of the trap, all the way at the back of the box. Near the scraps he put a small stick, which the skunk would have to hit while getting his meal. When the skunk disturbed the stick, a sliding door would shut behind him. At this point the skunk could not move. The box was small enough that he could not raise his tail to let loose his disagreeable charges of skunk odor.

Wayne placed the trap conveniently near the guest cabin. The kids were so anxious that he had to tell them not to stay near the trap. They went into the woods and watched quietly.

It didn't take too long before the trap was sprung and the children ran to Wayne with all the excitement you can imagine. Wayne walked out to the trap, threw it over his shoulder and started down toward the lake. He was like the Pied Piper being followed by all the children, and my dad and me also. Wayne walked out to the end of the dock and gradually lowered the box into the water. He held it there for some time. After a while he brought the box back up on the dock, opened the trap door and slid the dead animal into the water.

The box trap made the rounds with all the neighbors. Wayne built a couple more box traps so that everyone caught a good share of the skunk population around their cabins.

Wayne was always doing something around the cabin. He saw that our antique grandfather clock was not working. Dad had tried to get it fixed for years, but no one seemed to be able to fix it. Wayne told Dad he would like to see if he could find

With a (drowned) skunk

the problem. Believe it or not, he had every nut and bolt out of that clock on the table. My brother Dick was there at the time. He was a little trickster, and he placed some kind of a bolt in the mix Wayne had in the middle of the table. Wayne pondered this peculiar bolt and finally figured out it did not belong to the clock. Dick admitted he was having a little fun.

Wayne finally discovered that the problem was not in the workings. The movement of the clock hands was being impaired by the hands themselves, since they were quite large and locked themselves up. He asked my mother for a spool of thread. He removed the thread and formed a cylinder around the hands at the base to relieve the pressure. It worked! Needless to say, my dad had a different opinion of Wayne after that, almost to the point of thinking Wayne could do anything.

New Careers and Higher Learning

After my stint on the oil rig, winter was coming on. I wanted to pursue a licensed practical nurse course to further my knowledge in the healing arts. When I inquired about the LPN course at the hospital in Tulsa, they informed me the course was not available at that time. The nurse suggested that I might be interested in their aide course, which was about a three-week intensive. I accepted the opportunity and at the end of three weeks I was assigned to a floor.

Tulsa Hospital had 350 beds, with several floors and several stations to each floor. My station was the surgical station on the fourth floor. The hospital was run by Catholic nuns. It was a tight ship, very well managed. The nuns were totally dedicated to their work.

I enjoyed my job with its up and downs and sometimes tragedies. There was a young woman assigned to our floor with a terminal health problem. She had been a stewardess with the airline, and I remembered her. She fought the good fight, and I dropped in often to talk with her until she passed on.

There was an aide named Laura who had been with the hospital for about seven years. I had the feeling that I was encroaching on her territory, and I could feel a certain amount of animosity from her. The sisters often assigned me to their special patients (probably money donors), to whom Laura had generally been assigned. Perhaps it was because I was so well trained with the airlines and I loved to take care of people. The nun assigned to our wing, Sister Tibetha, may have encouraged the head nurse to assign me to some of these patients. Well, whenever I walked into the rest area for the aides at break time, everything was very quiet. I did feel the animosity, and I suspected that Laura was the instigator. But I never let it get to me—I was too busy.

My mother was a good teacher. She gave me wonderful lessons in loving people and how love can help those who have been particularly rude to others. She proved this time and time again, and here was my opportunity to work with the power of love.

Just a few months before I left the hospital, they decided to have representatives from each floor discuss general interaction with other floors so they could work together better in caring for patients. Each floor was to elect its own representative. By this time I was a ward clerk, which is a desk job, but working with the patients was still my favorite cup of tea. I approached Laura and told her I admired her work and I thought that she should represent our floor, since she had so many years of experience. I did not bat an eye and kept on talking, even though she looked like someone had hit her in the face with a dead fish. I told her that I was submitting her name to the committee for the vote, and that I was going to campaign for her.

I made posters and placed them all over the fourth floor, in all the wings. Laura now understood I was on her team and ready to help. She did not win the election, but our relationship did a 180-degree turn. In a short while I began preparing to move to Colorado. On my last day at the hospital, Laura came up to me and gave me a big hug.

Love *is* the magical key.

A fine specimen

Adventures in the High Country

$\mathcal{I}$n 1960, I concluded my three years with Tulsa Hospital. Wayne had been contacted by an oil promoter to move out to Gunnison, Colorado, our famous hunting grounds. The promoter was a big-time operator. He paid Wayne to bring the rig out to Colorado to explore the possibilities of finding oil. Either way, it was an opportunity to give it the old college try. After all, it was one of our favorite spots for hunting. Wayne accepted, and we were on our way. Wayne's old pilot buddy, Bart Cox, had a beautiful cabin on the Gunnison River. We had climbed many a mountain with Bart.

We moved into a trailer, and there was a lot of speculation about drilling sites. For myself, I had my sights set on the local hospital. I approached the head nurse, Stella Shaw, and told her about my hospital experience and working with a doctor. Gunnison had a 20-bed hospital, and it was not in the best of condition. Stella wanted to hire me but she could only pay me $2 an hour. I accepted. There were four doctors there who covered the small population of Gunnison, plus the little town to the north, Crested Butte, which had been a coal-mining town in its earlier days.

I was grateful for the job and more grateful that Stella trusted me. She started training me to work in the nursery, to help out in the emergency room and to circulate in the operating room. Since they did only spinals, all I did was get things they needed, talk to the patient and check blood pressure during the operation. Stella eventually trained me to work in the sterilization area to provide sterilized packs for operations and deliveries, and to check all the medical supplies in the delivery room, the operating room and the emergency room. That was my job two days a week. The other three days I was able to work with patients. By this time my pay had increased.

Within the year, they started building a new hospital around us while we were still in the old building. It was amazing to watch the construction, and soon we were in the new part without too many interruptions. We now had an X-ray room and an X-ray machine, which was woefully needed because of the potential broken legs coming from the newly famous Crested Butte ski area. We also had a radiologist who came to Gunnison once a month, when the hospital scheduled X-rays for people in this expanding area. The population always swelled in Gunnison during the fishing and hunting seasons. It also went up in the summers due to the many beautiful summer cabins and the tourism (which brought more incidents into the emergency room).

Dr. Burns, the radiologist, had his own plane and flew from Grand Junction, Colorado, into our little airport. I would pick him up early in the morning and take him back to the airport after his work was completed in the afternoon. He trained me to work with him, which was a pleasure and a great opportunity. He took the X-rays, and I helped arrange things and hold the patient if necessary. I wore a large apron to absorb any damaging rays from the X-ray machine. Following the X-ray sessions, Dr. Burns would check the X-rays and repeat his findings into a tape recorder for his secretary in Grand Junction. He wanted me to get the gist of his readings and take brief notes to give to the head nurse. The major reports were mailed back a day or two later. He was a very interesting man. I enjoyed working with him and talking to him through the years. He actually broke his own leg on the slopes of Colorado. I had a lot of fun with that one.

In 1967, I received a call that my father was not doing well, and I made arrangements to go to Minnesota. I arrived at the cabin to find my dear dad in a weakened condition. However, his mind was still as sharp as a tack. One morning as I was just arousing from sleep in the balcony area, I heard Dad getting up. He was talking on the telephone. Apparently he had been listening to the early morning market report and he was selling his stock. It was a regular thing with Dad to keep up with the market. I didn't pay too much attention until my sister called up later to tell Dad the stock market had dropped rather drastically. I told her he was way ahead of the game and had sold out early in the morning. He always said, "The little bird whistled." His little bird never let him down.

Within just a few days, Dad was not doing well at all and we took him to the hospital. He was very frail and bedridden, but his mind was always very clear. There were two other men also assigned to the same room at the hospital. The family made trips daily to see him.

One day I happened to be visiting Dad by myself and he

told me that he had had visitors that day. Of course I wanted to know who the visitors were. He told me that he saw three men in white standing behind a white fence, and the gate was open. He got the impression that he would be going through that gate, and that they were there to greet him. By this time I was pretty amazed, and I said, "Were you dreaming, Dad?" He retorted, "No, I was not dreaming!" He went on to say that it was so obvious to him that he was wondering if his roommates could see the apparition. But they were oblivious to the scene. By this time I was really excited for this wonderful experience given to him.

In the wee hours of the morning a few days later, Dad passed through that gate. He had everyone calm and collected for this great experience. There was sadness, of course, but there was the other equation that tells you of the great wonders of the beyond.

In the meantime, Wayne had decided to get into the water-well business, which was more lucrative than drilling for oil and helped pay the bills. It enabled us to purchase a very lovely log house with three bedrooms, a large living room, a fantastic fireplace, and a large kitchen with a little private office that Wayne used for his business. From the large windows in the living room there was a beautiful view of the mountains.

Since we had so much room, Wayne's mother, who was getting up in years, sold her house and came to live with us. My mother had been staying with my brother John, and we invited her to come to Gunnison for a change since we had a room for her, too. I got her interested in becoming a "gray lady" at the hospital. It was a great help to me, and it kept her busy. She was able to work with me in the sterilization room to help me set up packs and do other tasks that were menial for me and great for her.

The altitude in Gunnison is approximately 8,000 feet, and it is cradled in the mountains. Unfortunately, you had to come over a major pass from either direction, and we were prone to getting some heavy-duty accidents. If the patients' condition was very serious, we had to fly them out to the larger hospitals such as Grand Junction. For really serious problems, they went to Denver or Dallas. When we received the airlift cases I was the only one to go—everyone else was afraid to fly.

Rocky, our local bush pilot, had a single-engine craft. One patient was a young man who had been riding his motorcycle without a helmet. For some reason, he was thrown off the cycle onto some rocks and received a serious head injury. They kept him in Gunnison for a couple of days, and he never roused from the injury. I was concerned that they had not sent him out right away, it was that serious. Of course they finally did, and they asked me to go with Rocky and be with the patient.

I knew from experience that I needed restraints to keep the patient from moving about. With a head injury, the altitude creates pain to the head that can be excruciating. You know how your ears pop when you go up in altitude in a plane. It is the same idea, only far worse. I was to meet Rocky at the airport the next morning early, and we had a timetable to meet. I was there before the patient arrived. When they drove up with the patient, the first thing I asked for was the restraints. They had forgotten them, and I was not happy. I told Rocky to fly at the lowest possible altitude because we were headed over the high mountains to Dallas. This is not easy when you can suddenly hit downdrafts. It was not going to be a joyride.

Rocky did the best he could. I was sitting next to the patient, who was lying on a cot, and I had my hand on his torso in case he got edgy. I was beginning to feel his restlessness. The young man's feet were poised just behind Rocky's seat, because it was a small craft. The pain must have hit him in the head suddenly, because he braced his feet with such intensity that he broke a part of the pilot's seat. Rocky started getting pretty excited about this time, and at the same time the patient rose up and dove over the right front seat and reached for the door handle and was opening it. I was wrestling with a determined young man with all the strength that I had, and if it hadn't been for Rocky in the mix the patient might have gone out that door. The patient spent all of his energy and was exhausted by the time I got him back on the cot. Frankly, I was a bit weary too. I was amazed that he did what he did and thought that maybe there was some hope for him. He was obviously not a vegetable.

By this time, Rocky was well aware of keeping at a lower altitude. I was praying under my breath, for the trip was not over. With more miles behind us we could see the big city of Dallas. We helped transfer the patient to an ambulance, and that was a relief.

The trip back was the joyride, and the time to sightsee. Rocky spotted movement in the higher mountains and got closer. Elk were going single-file over some high, rugged mountains. There were hundreds of them, and they were quite fascinating to observe.

Trip to the British Isles

In 1969, not long after my dad passed, my brother John wanted to give my mother an opportunity to go to the British Isles for a bit of a break. He asked if I would go with her at his expense. Who could turn down a deal like that? Of course, I agreed to go.

Unfortunately, Wayne was upset that I would be leaving for about three weeks. He had been to England during the war and didn't have much good to say about it. I have a strong will, and I didn't get involved with his human explanations of why I should not go. I made my arrangements to leave.

My mother and I flew to Ireland. We were greeted at the Dublin airport, where we boarded a bus that took us to a hotel. The next morning we met about 38 others who had signed up for the trip. It was a congenial group of people, and we were together for the entire trip through the British Isles.

We did not tour Dublin at that time, but traveled by bus

to the southern part of the Republic of Ireland. We spent our nights in different places, and we traveled to large cities and towns that were unique and quaint. The Irish were dear, delightful people and very open to strangers. Their lifestyle seemed to be friendly and carefree.

Soon we were on our way back to Dublin, which had a whole different vibration. Tensions were high there, even as far back as that. However, we did see places of interest. One night we went to a nightclub where the entertainment was a group of Irish lasses and laddies with their beautiful singing voices and their Irish jigs. It was a refreshing show, but Dublin was a very heavy city as far as vibration.

A day or two later we boarded a boat that took us to Scotland. The sea was pretty choppy. Back on buses again, we traveled through Scotland, which was very scenic. We went by Loch Ness, the home of the famous monster, but fortunately he did not make an appearance. We went through the little town that my mother's father came from, and that was impressive. Next was the big city of Edinburgh. Edinburgh was an interesting city because it is old, yet its streets were wide. (Most of the towns in the British Isles had narrow streets.) We were warned that the crime rate was extremely high there and to be sure to walk in groups.

After that we traveled on toward Wales and spent the night in a castle that was really cold—it had hardly any heat. That was not our first castle (we had visited others as well), but it was the first one that had sleeping quarters. We went on to see the ancient Roman baths, and we eventually arrived in London. We saw Buckingham Palace, the statue of Thomas More, and Windsor Castle. You approached the castle on wide roads. Inside it was exquisite, with high ceilings and large rooms filled with gorgeous artifacts. The castle definitely exuded a sense of royalty.

In the meantime, my mother was feeling ill with chills and cold. We stayed cooped up in a hotel room, and I made sure she had everything she needed to recover before we made our return trip. We finally boarded a plane to New York. Mother returned to Minneapolis on one flight and I took another to my home.

As I was nearing Gunnison I hoped that all was well with Wayne. He seemed very happy to see me. Throughout the trip I had taken a lot of slides, which I shared with family and friends. Wayne also enjoyed the slide show.

It was a worthy trip and quite an adventure, thanks to Brother John.

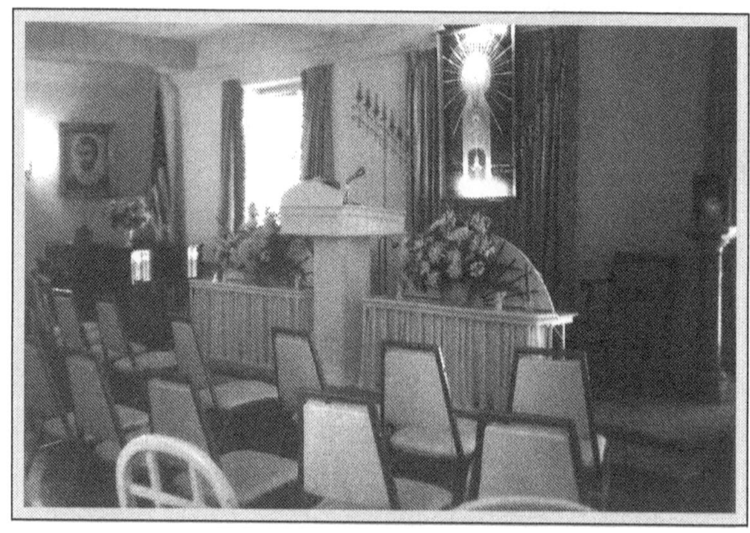

The chapel at La Tourelle

Part Five

"Where Truth Is"

Finding The Summit Lighthouse

*I*n the year 1971, Wayne and I went to Grand Junction to visit his Aunt Opal. Grand Junction was about 130 miles from Gunnison in the flatland area. Opal was in her seventies, and she was a total dear. We visited her frequently. She and I had become good buddies. I was never pleased with any of the churches in my area, and Opal and I often engaged in talks regarding esoteric teachings.

The week before our visit to Opal, I was outside washing windows. The sun was pretty intense, and I was a bit blinded. I was missing those wonderful esoteric books my dad had had. I called out to God in rather a determined manner and said, "Oh God, show me where Truth is!" I was bit shocked by my outburst.

Not long after that I was with Opal, who was smiling at me and saying, "I want you to read this." She handed me a Pearl of Wisdom from The Summit Lighthouse. When I was partly finished with the Pearl I asked her where it came from, and she told me to read on. The Pearl was signed by Mother Mary. I had known that Mother Mary was in the wings waiting for me. Now I had proof. Somehow I also knew instinctively that my appeal to God had been answered by Mother Mary.

Opal then told me about The Summit Lighthouse, which was located in Colorado Springs, on the other side of the mountains from Gunnison, where we lived. She also told me that she had signed up to be a Keeper of the Flame and she was now receiving their literature. I did not hesitate to sign up to be a Keeper too, for I knew this was the real thing. I too began receiving the wonderful Pearls. It was 36 years ago that I found my true path, and I have been grateful ever since.

I was told at that time that there was a family in Gunnison named Lowell who were long-time Keepers of the Flame, but I had not contacted them as yet. One day we had one of our serious accidents, and things did not bode well for the patient. I called up the Lowells and introduced myself, and they said they had heard about me. I asked them to pray for the patient, and they were going to get right to it. I called them back later to thank them for their prayer support and made arrangements to go to one of their weekly services.

I made it to a service, and that was my first contact with the science of the spoken Word. They played a dictation from one of the Masters. I was really impressed. I was well aware of the psychic world and mediums. They were always in a sleep vibration, which I was very leery of. The vibration of the dictation was amazing to me. Mark was always totally aware of what he was doing as he was speaking. It was genuine.

The words and works of the Masters are truly inspiring and full of profound wisdom of noble worth. Their teachings are like an implant—but it's up to you to become who you are. No one else can do it for you. You have to carve out your own destiny and rely on your God.

God really did answer my call, and the time was ripe for me to find the source of this gift.

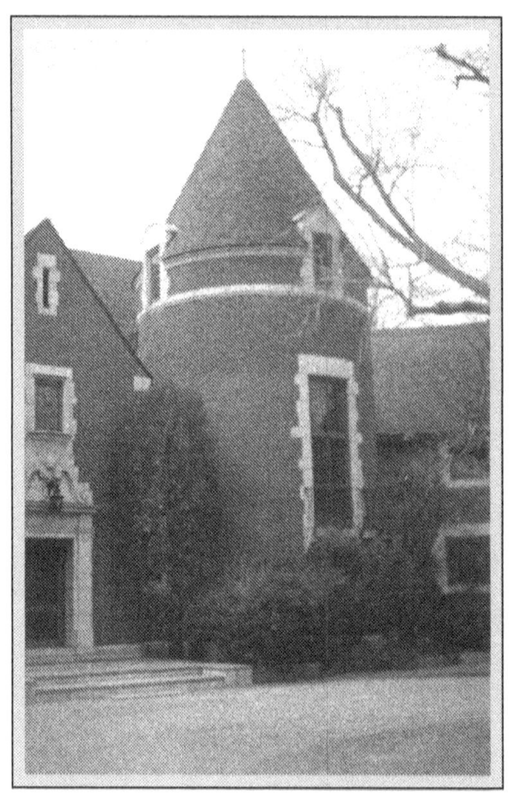

The tower where Mother worked

La Tourelle

$\mathcal{I}$n the fall of 1971, I made the 180-mile trip to The Summit Lighthouse at La Tourelle in Colorado Springs to be part of one of their quarterly conferences. The minute I walked into this beautiful mansion I was aware of the heavenly scent of roses. I thought it was incense, but when I mentioned it later I was told there was no incense burning anywhere in the building.

It was a thrill to be at the feet of the Masters speaking through the Messengers Mark and Elizabeth Prophet. Mark was truly a man of great stature, both by size and by the command of his aura. His lectures were profound, let alone the messages from the Masters. I always carried a pad and pencil, but I never took notes because I was so absorbed by Mark's words that I just listened intently.

Mark's lectures were laced with references to the evil that befalls men when they are unaware of conditions and circumstances created by the dark ones against the children of the light. It can be a tangled web of intrigue, unknown to the many. Mark's lectures would keep you totally engaged in listening; he was a master at delivering his message. He was quite aware of when his audience needed a little reprieve from heavy-duty subjects, and he would relax you with a funny story or joke. He had a great command of the English language. There is no question about it, he was an adept.

After the lecture, we gave decrees to prepare a platform of light to raise the consciousness of the congregation, to prepare us to receive the higher teachings from the Masters through the Messenger. We could see Mark looking to his left and then to his right as he spoke the Word. He explained to us later that he received the messages in words of living fire. The uplifting energy was felt by everyone, and the words were profound.

At one point I experienced an unusual phenomenon during a dictation: an unseen hand mysteriously sprayed a rose scent directly into my nostrils. It choked me to the point that I could hardly keep from coughing, which I knew would disturb the dictation. The lady who was sitting next to me told me later that she could smell the rose scent too, but only faintly. I could only surmise that my aura needed cleaning up—who knows? Later on when I became a staff member, I encountered that same rose scent now and then at the Motherhouse in Santa Barbara. It did not dawn on me until now that it must have been Mother Mary, because rose is her scent. Better late than never, when you recognize the power of the light that surrounds us!

Elizabeth (who is now called "Mother" per one of the Masters) gave dictations also. Hers were generally taken "ex cathedra": the Master stands within the aura of the Messenger and uses her vocal cords to speak while she remains fully conscious. It took many years of rigorous training to accomplish this feat. She realized that she had to shed a lot of the human concepts that we all indulge in, and obey immediately. It was this obedience in even menial tasks assigned to her by El Morya that created the vessel by which she became an instrument for the light. She always obeyed immediately.

Someone explained to me that when you wear jewelry while listening to dictations in the presence of the Masters, the gems and gold come out looking highly polished. The next time I went back to La Tourelle, I remembered to wear one of two gold bracelets that once belonged to my grandmother. After my return from that conference I discovered that the one I had worn was bright and shiny, while the other lacked luster. The one I had worn had obviously gone through an alchemical change.

At one point on one of my trips to Colorado Springs for a conference, there was a break at the end of a session. People had gone outside for a breath of fresh air. As for me, I was wandering around this lovely mansion, and I opened the door to the Blue Room, which I had been aware of before. Mark was standing in the middle of the room as I opened the door. I was totally surprised. I cannot explain the eye contact, but it was electrifying. It seemed like Mark knew I would be entering the room. I graciously apologized for the disturbance and closed the door. I shall never forget that moment.

Fortunately I was able to travel to La Tourelle a few times before Mark had his stroke and was taken to the hospital in February 1973. There was severe damage to the brain and they had to put him on a life support system, as he could not breathe on his own. Mother told us later that she was communicating at inner levels with him, and she knew that she had to disconnect the life support. On February 26, 1973, Mark Prophet made his transition and swiftly ascended. Now Mother had a great challenge ahead as the sole Messenger for the Great White Brotherhood and the head of The Summit Lighthouse. She also had four small children who were now fatherless. This was an enormous challenge, and she faced it with great courage.

I was in Gunnison working at the hospital when I received the news. Mother was asking everyone who could to come to a special service for our beloved Mark. Everyone who was coming was asked to fast and pray. Mother was going to perform the service herself. All the staff members came, plus quite a few Keepers of the Flame from around the area.

At the service Mother wore Mark's blue robe, and it nearly swallowed her up. She gave a beautiful ceremony but you could sense the strain. She blessed everyone she could, starting with the staff and then all the familiar old-timers.

George Lancaster was one of those old-timers. He was a little on the heavy side and arthritic. Mother had a pillow on the floor for people to kneel on. George had a little bit of a struggle in kneeling, and she was assisting him. She laid her hands on him and said, "George, you can ascend in this life." We had been taught that you could win your ascension, but it was not in my realm of thinking at that time. For Mark, yes, he was an adept. But right then and there I decided that I was going to catch up with that little man and get to know him. It took a few years before I did, which I will convey to you in another part of this book.

In the spring of 1973, the Easter conference was a must for me, and I made all manner of preparations to make sure I got there. It was unbelievable how many people attended. The sanctuary was filled to capacity, and every large room throughout the mansion was also filled to capacity with many chairs and speaker set-ups for each room. It was quite an exciting time and an electrifying experience. It was obvious that Mark had radiated his divine energy to many people who were supposed to be with this activity. La Tourelle was about to burst at the seams.

Mother had Mark's blue robe on again, and she must have had some tucks taken here and there because it fit her a little bit better. It was during this conference that Mother introduced us to the Cosmic Clock. She formed a clock circle with its twelve lines and asked people to come up in groups of twelve. Many groups were formed. Each group was asked to take one of the lines of the clock with its different attributes. I happened to end up on the 10 o'clock line, which is God-vision. That ceremony was very impressive and poignant—one you wouldn't forget even in your old age.

Mother took advantage of the great light that was released by the whirlwind action of the ascension of Mark Prophet, now called Lanello. With this in mind, she called to many of the hierarchs of heaven to do the mighty work of God for the world through this large conference. Mother was making all kinds of fiery invocations, but at one moment she started to giggle. She composed herself and said she would tell us later what had happened. In the meantime she was witnessing and describing a scene of Archangel Michael going into the astral plane to release angels who were trapped there. She described the scene vividly, and the angels were released with the help of our decrees as well. They were called the Restored Angels. We were told that we could call on them at any time, and they would help us in our own invocations for life on planet Earth. I keep them pretty busy.

One wonders how an angel can get trapped. How faithful

they are to our lifestreams! They go the extra mile and then some. They are the ever-ready servants of God. We do know the call compels the answer, and help does come from the higher octaves of light instantly.

We finally reminded Mother about the part she was going to tell us. She described the scene: there were elementals all over the place, and they were tugging on her garments and saying, "Mother, don't forget us!" Of course, they were also included in the release of light.

I learned later about an incident that happened in the children's program, which was being held in a separate building, the gate house. When a mother came to pick up one of the children, he described the scene of Archangel Michael going into the astral plane just as Mother had described it. The mother heard the story firsthand again from her son, and she was flabbergasted. They had to admit that he saw what he saw and it could not be denied. I have always said that truth is stranger than fiction.

Conference Time at the Land of Lanello

By this time my family was getting used to my going off to conferences now and then. Now I was planning for the big one, which would be about a two-week stint: the July conference of 1973.

Some time before Mark passed on, he bought a large piece of acreage located about 40 miles northwest of Colorado Springs, possibly to build on or as an investment. It was quite a nice area with mountains and valleys. They decided that it would be suitable for the Fourth of July conference. It would be a tent city, with a very large tent for the main conference, smaller tents for food, showers and bathroom facilities, and last but not least, dormitory tents for the men and for the women. It was obvious they had to get a big space because more and more people were finding the teachings. No doubt Lanello was getting his flock together at inner levels.

The conference was announced well ahead of time and

the Keepers did a lot of work helping to advertise it. I did my share in the town of Gunnison and I made sure the conference posters were seen in many storefronts.

The conference, which lasted four days, was outstanding. I can still remember some of the things the Masters and Cosmic Beings presented to us. An unprecedented 21 dictations were given through Mother. No doubt Lanello's light energy from his ascension gave her the tremendous impetus to accomplish this amazing feat. About a thousand people attended this affair, and the science of the spoken Word was used very powerfully. Mother has said that the power of the spoken Word released through the decrees is the backbone of this organization.

After the main event was concluded, there was a ten-day wilderness training that was given by a group from the Mormon Church. This was a great opportunity for anyone interested in what you can do for your family in case of catastrophe—war, famine or nature's upheaval. Aunt Opal came for the whole show, and she was quite a trooper.

I took all ten days of the wilderness training, and it was very worthwhile. I even learned how to rappel off the side of a mountain. The Mormons are well prepared for all sorts of disasters. They advise you to have dried food and water at your disposal for any kind of disaster.

A dictation from one of the Masters explained (and I am paraphrasing) that the balance of light becomes difficult to sustain in the physical world when there is so much darkness. Old records accumulate until an imbalance is created, and the Elohim need to make adjustments to the planet's axis. At that time, the Master told us, the axis of the earth was at the point of a wobble and adjustments had to be made. When adjustments come, cataclysm follows.

I was very impressed by this statement, and it was uppermost in my mind. Not too long after I returned home there was an article in the paper about an earthquake in South America that devastated a large area. About 10,000 people lost their lives. I was even more surprised to find in the newspaper about a week later that the earth's axis had adjusted itself so-and-so many degrees. I was so excited to have proof positive of God's work through the higher beings making adjustments for the planet that I mentioned it to my family. It did not change their thinking, and I had the feeling they thought I might be "out to lunch," as the saying goes.

The Keepers of the Flame are the doers. We must be responsible to gather as groups across the many nations and be as one voice shouting in the wilderness of civilization. As Mother stated, it only takes a few to stand up and be heard by the power of the decree. Our job is to keep on keeping on. Each of us who knows the truth must stand up, make the call, and hold the balance by the very Word itself.

At that July conference the Goddess of Liberty inaugurated Ascended Master University, which was going to be a three-month course. I was so impressed that I absolutely knew I had to go. The "how" did not enter my mind, but I knew it was for me.

The Motherhouse

My Determination

$\mathcal{I}$n the fall of 1973, I was trying to figure out the how for attending Ascended Master University. The first AMU was going on at this time at the Motherhouse in Santa Barbara, California. I was pretty frustrated, and I had told the Lowells that I simply did not have $2,000 to cover the tuition, room and board.

In the meantime Wayne needed to go to Grand Junction, and I went along to see Aunt Opal. When I told her of my dilemma, she immediately told me that she had $2,000 to give me. I refused, but she wouldn't take no for an answer. She insisted that I take her offer. I told her I didn't know when I could pay her back. She did not want me to be concerned about it. Through this sweet lady the possibility became a reality.

Communicating with my family was not going to be easy. I reflected back on the time after my dad passed, when my brother John sent me with my mother to the British Isles. Making my plans to go to AMU was an entirely different situation.

By this time it was the season to head for the hills for hunting, and Wayne was making all sorts of preparations to go. I told him very gently that I would not be going up that year, and he was surprised and disappointed. He left for the camp. When he had been gone for a while, I approached my mother and told her that I was thinking about going to AMU for three months. She actually went ballistic, and I was so shocked that I dared not approach the subject again.

That night I went to bed with a heavy heart. I felt my hopes were dashed. The dream that interrupted my sleep was a real nightmare. I was very aware that everybody was unhappy with me and that I was causing problems. At this point I woke up. I was sitting at the side of my bed sobbing, when suddenly I felt an electric shock go through my entire body. I was infused with the determination to go to AMU. Since I was such a devotee of Saint Germain, I think it was a special alchemy for me to be on my way. I knew that it had to be done without anyone knowing, and I prepared myself the next day for a journey I knew I had to take.

I had given notice at the hospital a few weeks before, so they could plan for a replacement while I was gone. I had planned ahead, but I hadn't yet approached the subject. Now the subject was signed, sealed and delivered to me. Soon I had everything packed that I thought I would need. I left late in the evening after my mother had gone to bed. I had made arrangements to stay with the Lowells for the night and to leave from there early the next morning for Aunt Opal's home in Grand Junction. I left a note for my family asking for them to understand and saying that I would be back and that

I would be in touch with them.

Before I left for the long journey I wanted to stop over at Grand Junction to get the car tuned up for the trip to Santa Barbara. I was grateful to spend the next night with Opal, and she was very excited for me to be going to AMU. The next day fairly early in the morning the phone rang, and I just knew it was Wayne. I told Opal I was stepping outside so that she could say I was not there. Not long after that, I was headed for California.

I traveled until it was dark. Then I turned up a side street in a little town and curled up in the back seat for a nap. I reached the coast the next day and found a reasonable hotel in Santa Barbara. It was mid-November, and I got a job working in a nursing home to help pay for my expenses.

Destiny has its drawbacks, and I got very ill with a fever. I was in bad shape, and I knew I needed help. I called Patricia Johnson, whom I had met at a conference in October. She came right over, picked me up and took me to the apartment she shared with her son Kerry and Evelyn Dykman. Both Patricia and Evelyn have since made their ascension. It is a comfort to know you have such friends in the octaves of light.

It was a very large apartment. Patricia's bedroom had twin beds, and she invited me to stay in her room. The next day I went to the emergency room at the local hospital. The doctor said that I had pneumonia and that I needed a shot of penicillin, which I dutifully took. That night I woke up with the strangest feeling. I knew I was in trouble when my air intake was difficult and I felt swollen. I went into the bathroom, and one look in the mirror convinced me I needed to get to the emergency room fast. My eyes were almost swollen shut, and my cheeks were even with my nose. I was allergic to the penicillin!

I went to the bedroom door, and without turning on the lights I explained to Patricia that I had a problem and I didn't want her to be alarmed. I turned on the lights and she couldn't help laughing when she saw my funny face. I agreed with her, and I added that I probably should get to the emergency room to stop the swelling. I asked if Kerry would take me there, and he did.

By this time it was difficult to breathe, and they immediately gave me all kinds of shots to reverse the swelling. One of them was adrenalin to make sure my heart would pump fast to speed up the action to counteract the penicillin. At that point I thought my heart was coming out of my chest and I would burst at the seams. They kept me in the emergency room until I stabilized. When the swelling started dissipating, I returned to the apartment with Kerry. The next day I broke out in hives, and that was a siege in itself. I was highly sensitive to anything at this point. My immune system was not up to par.

With the help of the Johnsons and Evelyn, I was about ready to take on AMU. In the meantime I had called my family and explained my problem. Wayne was very kind and sent me some much-needed money for all the expenses I had incurred by the trips to the emergency room and the drugs I was taking. He always had a sweet heart.

Ascended Master University

elieve it or not, I made it. I went to the second quarter of AMU, sponsored by Lord Lanto, in the winter of 1974.

There were 76 students assigned two to a room at the Towers, a hotel located right on the ocean half an hour or so from Santa Barbara. The ocean looked great, but I never had the opportunity to take a dip at that beach. We were bused to the Motherhouse daily. On Saturdays it got to be customary for the men and women to sit on the floor at the elevator area on the women's floor, which was quite large, and go over our notes together for the tests that followed the weekend. This truly was a great opportunity to compare what we had gleaned, and we had some great discussions on the teachings.

It felt good to be back at the Motherhouse, but I had a problem due to a residue of a cough. Because Mother's lectures were being recorded, I had to sit just outside the double doors to the classroom, in a long hallway. The main entrance into the building from the street was about midway down this hallway. Mother's private office was in this same hallway near the classroom on the side of the entrance from the street. Across from the main entrance were double glass doors, plus very large windows that extended the whole length of the hallway on the side away from the street. Those windows opened into a beautiful backyard with a slight hill at the far end and lovely shrubs and flowers around the sides. It was a very lush scene, and there was a feeling of openness as you entered the hallway.

Mother's lectures were very interesting and extremely important. Once when Mother started talking about Mark, she suddenly choked up and excused herself from the podium. She went immediately to her office. As she passed me, I could see the tears in her eyes. At that moment I felt like I had to be Mother's champion, and this feeling is still with me now, 33 years later.

Every Sunday we had a dictation. Some Sundays we traveled to other areas and had dictations in large rooms at hotels. If there were Keepers in the local area, they were welcome to come.

During the class we did exorcisms in Los Angeles and San Francisco. The one in Los Angeles, our first exorcism, was quite interesting. The Cosmic Clock is a key to many avenues of infinite purpose. It is a science in itself, and for this purpose we were going after the negative aspects from the 12 o'clock line back to the 12 o'clock line. We had to decide where the center of Los Angeles was located. Mother tuned in to the very famous Rose Garden. From that point we looked at the perversions of the areas of Los Angeles that some students were aware of, according to the lines of the clock. It all fell into place, starting at the 12 o'clock line.

After Mother gave an invocation, the bus moved away from the Rose Garden. We made our first stop at the 12 o'clock line for our clearance calls and continued on to all the other lines that were plotted out. When we came to the 4 o'clock line (the line of disobedience), I was feeling very ill and could hardly concentrate on what we were trying to do. When we got back to the 12 o'clock line it all cleared up. I could only imagine it must have been a long-ago record of my own, or perhaps a heavy-duty record from some activity in that area. This exorcism was a real hands-on experience, and I was grateful to be a part of it.

One of my outstanding memories is when Mother came into the classroom and told us it was time to go after Lucifer. Apparently he had physically attacked her—we were not told how. He had been one of the highest angels in heaven known to us, until his pride took over. That attainment came to an end when he rebelled thousands of years ago, claiming he was the all-powerful one. He took a third of the angels with him. The Bible says that he was cast out of heaven and his angels were cast out with him. Mark and Mother were never permitted to go after Lucifer because of the attainment he still had at the time when they were together. Lucifer did attempt to cause trouble for them, but working for the Great White Brotherhood they were protected.

Meanwhile Lucifer had been losing attainment, and Mother had been gaining attainment. They were now at the same level, and she was able to begin to do battle with him. His attack on her was his last hurrah. Mother was very aware of him raging up and down the Pacific coast at this time. Our winter quarter of AMU had a classroom full of chelas who were ready to enter the fray with Mother as our fearless leader. We did many hours of calls to Astrea's circle and sword of blue flame. When we went outside that day for a fresh-air break, there was a cloud in the sky that caught our attention. It was a huge, circular white cloud with a sword thrust through the center of the circle. We were often told that nature outpictures what is going on in the vicinity, and the sylphs of the air had outdone themselves on this one.

It was nearing the end of AMU, and I was preparing in my mind to get ready to go back to Colorado. I had kept in touch with the family. In the meantime my mother had returned to Minnesota with my brother John.

Some of the AMU students were applying for staff jobs, and I decided to do the same thing. I was planning on it being temporary. Annice Booth suggested I temporarily take over the phones for Mother's secretary, Nancy Priest [Johnson]. She was swamped with phone calls, and any kind of relief would be a big help. I accepted and found myself in a little room with "Uncle" Kenneth McNeel. Kenneth traveled all over the world and had the ability to buy the most beautiful and expensive jewelry. At this time he was the book stocker and seller for the Motherhouse. We shared an office just off the kitchen, which had been a utility room. At one time used for dishes, glasses, trays, et cetera, now it was filled with books and the two of us. There were two doors, one into the dining room (the Blue Room) and the other into the kitchen. It was not a large facility by any means, but Kenneth and I happened to work quite well with cramped quarters. My desk faced the freeway between the two doors. I can assure you that it often had traffic. Fortunately there was a high window that let in lots of light, and I could see the clouds and the treetops. Who could ask for more?

My car was in pretty good shape and occasionally Mother would ask me to take her to her downtown office, which was a more private area for her to do her work for the Brotherhood. At that time she was working on the book *Quietly Comes the Buddha*. On one occasion she had me drive her to an antique shop. I couldn't find a parking spot, and Mother had me drop her off so I could park farther down the street. I was a bit concerned because it was not the best part of town. There were no parking spots, and there was no way to turn around for a few blocks. I finally was able to turn and head back up the street near where I left Mother, and I found a parking spot. I was walking toward the shop when I saw Mother heading right for me. I apologized and told her my parking problem and said I was sorry I couldn't get back sooner since this was not the best part of town. She immediately retorted, "Don't you think these people need my light too?" I learned a big lesson, and I appreciated Mother more and more. It was not a prideful answer, by any means. It was an answer from one who cares for all people.

I was really torn up deciding whether or not to go home to Wayne. One day I stayed home from work, and I think I cried all day about the situation. At one point I was driving Mother around and I dropped her off at her house. I was helping gather up some items for her, and I asked if I could ask her a question. She said, "Of course you may." The question was, did I need to go back with my family. Her answer was short and to the point: "Remember Gautama Buddha?" Yes, I did remember the sacrifice he made when he left his wife and infant son. He knew his mission was to find Truth and to help mankind also find that Truth. That is all it took, and I am still with The Summit Lighthouse.

One day Mother asked me if I would mind coming over in the mornings about 6 a.m. to hold the balance for her and her family. Tatiana was a small baby at the time. I immediately responded that I would. To me it was a great honor. I have always been an early riser and I still rise very early. One morning I was at the bottom of the stairs in the chair that Mother had suggested I sit in to do the decrees. Suddenly I was aware of Mother at the top of the steps with Tatiana in her arms. She had a robe on, and she looked like the Madonna with child. I shall never forget that scene.

AMU continued in Santa Barbara for a while, and Mother also had second quarter for more advanced studies. In 1975, we moved to Colorado Springs to set up what was now being called Summit University (SU). The Motherhouse remained as a focus for the Keepers of the Flame for a few years. Meanwhile, back in Colorado Springs they were trying to make arrangements to accommodate a larger body of students. They rented a large complex called the Château Motor Hotel, from which they could easily bus students back and forth. It had a hundred rooms, upper and lower stories, in a U-shaped configuration with a swimming pool at the end of the U. It had lovely grounds with trees, flowers and shrubs, and a large dining room just above the office area. We had our own great cooks, and wonderful food was provided for the students. Several of the staff had rooms there, with two staff members to a room. The others remained at La Tourelle.

Werner Zotter and I were co-managers for the motel. Somebody had to always man the desk, since some rooms were available to the public. As for me, I was available to jump in and get the work done when necessary. The students took care of their own rooms. It was a good arrangement at the time.

Ruthie Jones, a long-time staff member, had been a schoolteacher and worked with both Mark and Mother over the years. She was always working with the children, and

I believe she wrote some children's books. She was stricken with cancer and was at the point where she had to be placed in the hospital. Several of us would drop in to see her, and she always remained cheerful. Her favorite words were always "Remember, love is the key!"

In her final days, she was placed in a small nursing home, where she passed on peacefully. Mother was there by her side and witnessed that she had taken her ascension on the inner. Mother called all the staff to come down because the radiation that was transmitted in the physical was very apparent. We all obeyed immediately and made our way to the nursing home. There must have been at least 30 of us, and the old folks from the home were really curious. Most of them were "nodders" sitting in their chairs, but they were wide awake that day wondering what on earth was going on. Mother had us line up in single file and go quietly into the room in groups of seven, and just meditate for a period of time. The vibration was amazing, and you could sense a sweet holiness.

In 1976, Summit University classes were getting larger. It was decided that we needed to find a bigger space and better accommodations. They found an ideal campus in Pasadena, California, which was vacant and available for lease. It had many business offices and a large campus, sleeping quarters and auditoriums. It fitted our needs and we prepared to move to Pasadena.

This time my car headed back to California with a couple of extras on board. We were all anxious to find a spot where we could expand and have a larger group of people. We were creating a vacuum to be filled and it was filled. We had easily 400-plus attendees for the next conference. Each conference from then on increased in size.

The hills of Pasadena

Pasadena, California

The Pasadena campus was quite an expansive area with a large administration building. One of the buildings had a large kitchen and dining area at the basement level, with windows that allowed the light to come in. It could hold a large crowd. There was also a dispensary in this complex. The campus included several dorms and two auditoriums, one that held 200 people and the other around 2,500 people. Across the campus in low-lying buildings were classrooms for children, suitable for all grades needed for our staff children and their teachers.

Soon I was back to my original job as phone operator. It was now a 24-hour operation, and that made me the supervisor for the telephone services. I set up slots to cover the hours. I was the operator during the day, but I also became the housing manager. I assigned the staff their rooms and had a master plan as to where everyone was assigned.

In 1976 we were beginning to prepare for a large conference. Mother decided to let people sleep on the floor for free, since they were paying for the class. She suggested that families might want to stay in the smaller auditorium in family groups. In another building there were actually some beds available, which were also free. My job was to have all the names assigned on a chart, and I had to monitor the spaces and places. This was one of the most interesting jobs I ever had, and I might say one of the most challenging, too. Believe me, every conceivable space was used. There were two long floors in the big building, one floor above the other, and I marked off spaces with chalk. One floor was for men and the other was for women. I assigned each space, and it seemed to come out quite even.

This story was related to me not too long ago by Svend Anderson, who shared a room with three other men. It seems I was going around checking the rooms I had assigned to make sure all was well. In one of the rooms I had assigned Svend and another older gentleman to the two beds. When I knocked on the door, to my surprise the two young men were in the beds and the gentlemen were on the floor. "You and you, on the floor," I ordered, in top sergeant style. "Those beds are for the older gentlemen"—and they knew it. Svend told me the young men really scrambled off the beds and did what was required of them. I don't remember anything about the episode, but I did conclude it helps to have a little authority once in a while.

The housing situation worked out well, and we had a capacity crowd in the large auditorium. Mother gave lectures, and she would often show slides. One time during a lecture a key slide was missing, and the operator of the projector was at a loss to find it. Suddenly it appeared on the screen. It seems that Mother saw Lanello cross the stage, and the slide mysteriously appeared. It pays to have an Ascended Master around, as she told us later.

Pasadena has a large number of fundamentalist churches, and one day in 1977 a group of marchers surrounded the property with very uncomplimentary signs and unpleasant energy. They depicted us pretty much as the devil. Fortunately, we were in the process of securing our own property in a very lovely area near Malibu. It had everything we needed, including a main chapel, a smaller chapel, lots of buildings and plenty of space.

Main entrance to the Grail building

Camelot Come Again

$\mathcal{I}$n 1978, we were ready to move to the new campus. Some of us stayed in Pasadena, and I remained on the phones there for a later move. They had a phone system at the new campus, and they had someone answering the phones there as well.

Camelot was the perfect place for our growing staff and for expanding our publications. As I remember, it was about seven miles to the ocean, a very beautiful winding drive mostly downhill from the campus. Camelot had been a private estate with rolling hills and beautiful trees. The original mansion overlooked a small lake. The Catholics had bought the estate and added their lovely features, including the two chapels. As you entered the property there was a gate with an arch, and beyond that a long paved road lined with trees on both sides. As you continued down the road, you drove under an arch-way that was attached to large buildings on either side, with an overhead hallway between them. Past that point you were in a circular driveway, with several buildings positioned on the outer rim of the circle.

Within the circular drive was a circular lawn with a large statue of Jesus with his arms outstretched, facing the main building that contained the larger chapel, the Chapel of the Holy Grail. As you walked into the main entrance of the Grail building, you were in a long hallway that extended to other rooms.

Immediately across from the main doorway were two large doors into the expansive chapel. It had high ceilings and stained-glass windows depicting saints. The altar was very impressive. The chapel seated around 350, and there was a choir loft in the back. On either side of the altar was a major entrance. On the left side was the sacristy, where Mother prepared for the services. The opposite side was the entrance to the AV area, where they controlled the sound. They also had a video camera set up in front of the platform. The acoustics were excellent in that chapel, and we were awed by the many dictations that were given there.

Back to the hallway: the extended corridor had large windows with lovely views on both sides. At the end of the hall was a large room that seated at least 150 people. This was used for overflow, for staff meetings and for special forums. Mother established Summit University Forum events, with very interesting guest speakers on a variety of fascinating subjects, some controversial. These forums were very informative and highly interesting.

Beyond this end of the building was what was once the carriage house for the mansion. It housed our AV technicians and their offices. The AV department supplied the Keepers of the Flame with tapes and albums of Mother's lectures and dictations from the Masters. They were a very busy crew.

Back where you entered the circle at the archway was a very large building to the right, which we called the Mansion. It was so large that it extended around the circle somewhat. A great deal of this building, if not all, was probably the major part of the original mansion.

To name a few of its many functions, this is where Mother's living quarters and office were. Mother had an office upstairs, where she loved to work because of the quietude. The lower quarters housed various officials and their secretaries. It had a large veranda in what would be the front of the building, with a view of a broad, sweeping lawn that sloped down to the lake. The lawn and the Mansion were shaded by beautiful leafy trees, and there were swans on the lake.

The veranda had another door to the right, which opened into the office of Edward Francis's secretaries. You entered Edward Francis's office from his secretaries' area. His personal office had windows with a view of the lake. Back to the veranda again: there were two large doors in the middle of this rather large veranda. As you entered this room, what stood out was a large fireplace. On either side of the fireplace were two doors that took you out to that circular road. This room was a major location for many events.

There was much more going on in this building. The high school was at the far end. It had quite a few students. The front of the building, at ground level facing the lake, housed a fairly large store that stocked all manner of items, including our publications.

Alongside this building was a lovely walk to the Novitiate. There was a swimming pool to the left of the walk about midway. As you approached the Novitiate, the first building was another beautiful high-ceilinged chapel that held about a hundred people. It was called the Chapel of the Holy Family. We used this chapel often for introductory programs for new people who were interested in the teachings. The staff used it for various functions as well, including meetings with Mother.

The cafeteria was located in the same building, next to the chapel. You could eat inside or outside on the patio. As you continued down the long hallway there were more offices. Last but not least were the dorm rooms for men on one side and for women on the other side.

Also in this building we would eventually house our beloved Madame Elisabeth Caspari, a student and friend of the Italian doctor and educator Maria Montessori. Dr. Montessori trained and tutored Madame Caspari during World War II, when they were both stranded in India. Madame Caspari was eager to come to the United States to teach the Montessori method. This method helps preschoolers learn to work independently, to make choices and to carefully return the many training materials to the shelves in proper order. When you walk into a Montessori classroom, the children are busy doing a variety of hands-on work.

Madame Caspari found the teachings of the Masters and came to Camelot. She moved to Montana when we moved. She was our very own beloved lady, who passed on not long ago at the age of 102. She trained many of our people from all over the country in the Montessori method, some of whom later established schools in various parts of Montana and elsewhere. She was charming and gracious, and we all learned from this special soul. When she made her transition, the chapel was full for her memorial service, and the comments regarding her were many because all had wonderful memories of this special teacher of love. She was a gentle soul.

Our first major ceremony at Camelot, after we settled down, was a grand march from the front gate with the permanent staff carrying the artifacts from the church in Pasadena that were to be arranged in their proper places in the new chapel. Margaret Reichardt and I were assigned to carry the "blazing Shiva" statue that was placed at the front of the altar near the steps going up to the altar.

Oddly enough, I was to take over Margaret Reichardt's job as the personnel manager about two years down the line. Margaret's main job became working with Florence Miller, who was the shining light of the graphic arts department.

Florence was a personal friend and confidante to Mother. At this time Florence was suffering with severe headaches. She often had to lie down on the couch in her office and continue to work from there. Unfortunately, her headaches went on for months. Eventually they found the cause, which was an inoperable tumor at the base of her skull. In 1979, our beloved Florence Miller ascended from this life and left a legacy for all to follow in her footsteps. She is now called the Ascended Lady Master Kristine. We couldn't have a finer friend in heaven, as well as the many others who ascended from this organization.

Because we had so many staff members and Summit University was still a three-month course, we needed a bigger facility for housing for all. The church rented a large facility that was about a 40-minute drive down the coast. We called it Camp Victory. There were adequate rooms and plenty of showers, and it was actually pretty comfortable. We had one man who kept the camp in shape, cleaned the restrooms, and did all the support work for the good-sized facility. With everyone gone during the day, one person could get the job done. The students and staff took care of their own private areas. There was an inspection now and then by me.

My salary was not adequate for all the expenses I had incurred. Dr. Ralph Yaney and his wife, Lucille, offered me a one-day-a-week job helping them run the gift shop at their restaurant in Topanga Canyon. This is a very popular eating place with many in that area and beyond. It was a saving grace for me, and I really enjoyed those years. The restaurant is still thriving at this date of 2007.

There was one particular incident that occurred on my watch early one morning at the telephones. I received a call from the Washington, D.C., Teaching Center regarding a possible plot to blow up the Washington Monument. This particular monument is one of the sustaining talismans for the United States. I knew that this was serious and that Mother needed to be informed ASAP. This was early in the morning and I called five major people to be sure Mother got this message. I could not let this slip through the cracks.

Mother happened to call a little later in the morning. I asked her if she had received the message, and she had not. I was shocked that no one had informed her. Soon she had all six of us standing before her in her office. We were told again about the importance of that monument. Mother admonished me for not picking up the phone and calling her directly at home, and she was absolutely correct. From that time on I informed Mother directly and sometimes overly informed her. As far as I am concerned, the chastisements were well worth it, because chastisement cleaves the unreal from the Real swiftly.

The Montessori High School students were a very talented group, and they put on some great plays. They had songs and dances and produced their own plays. They formed a band and learned to march together, and they performed at one of the stadiums in downtown Los Angeles, with all the trimmings and colorful uniforms. They entertained us a great deal and it was terrific. We were all very proud of them.

Early in 1980 I was contacted by Margaret Reichardt and informed that Mother wanted me to take over Margaret's personnel responsibilities. After Florence Miller passed on, Margaret had received the mantle of the graphics department and no doubt was overly burdened. My comment to her was, "Margaret, I am not a secretary." That did not work. Margaret told me that all I would be doing was storing the files and keeping them in order. HO! HO! HO! I can honestly tell you I really dragged my heels on this one, and I was not exactly passing my test.

About two weeks went by and Margaret said that Mother wanted me to take over for her as soon as possible. So the personnel office ended up in my personal room with a couple of file drawers. On top of this, it was decided that I would be making photo IDs for the staff. So I now had a large camera in my room. In the meantime a big office with three rooms opened up for me, right next to the phone room. The best part was that there was a connecting storage room for both areas. I never had it so good, except I needed a secretary badly due to the fact that I was still an operator, tag coordinator and housing manager. They sent me one of the best secretaries on staff, Diana Winn [Good]. The breakdown of the word secretary is "secret ray," and Diana always got the job done.

My interaction with Mother increased. My job was working not only with the current staff but also with new people who wanted to apply for staff positions. I was now handling the files of possible new staff and interviewing those who had gone to SU and wanted to join staff. After all the folders and interviews were completed, Mother would call me into the sacristy and review each folder and ask questions. She trusted my judgment, and soon our staff began to grow.

About this time, I was able to fulfill my desire to get to know George Lancaster. He had moved to Long Beach, California, probably after we left the Colorado area. He had been a bartender at one time and I am not sure when he found the teachings. But he did know Mother and Mark and was very close to them. As I mentioned before, after the memorial service for Mark when Mother was giving the blessings for those who were close to Mark, she said, and I quote, "George, you can ascend in this life." I said at the time that I wanted to catch up with this little guy and get to know him.

Soon after we arrived at Camelot, George started showing up. One day I did catch up with George and got acquainted with him. We struck up a great friendship, and we got together frequently when George came to services. At that time I had my big camera upstairs, and one day the moment was right to ask him to come upstairs so that I could get his picture. When we got up there, just before I took the picture I said, "George, you are going to ascend in this life," and when he had that big grin I took the picture. That picture was eventually used for a Keepers' Lesson.

One day I received a call from George from Long Beach, and he was very upset. He had had a slight stroke, and his son had put him in a nursing home. He was almost in tears. I told George we were coming down to see him as quick as we could. I contacted Mother and told her what had happened and that George was very despondent. She immediately made arrangements for four of us to go down and see George the next day.

It took us about one and a half hours to get to Long Beach. The nursing home was not the best. We found George seated in a wheelchair in a large room by himself with his back to us. I walked around and said, "George, we have arrived," and he broke down and cried. Somehow we got him interested in getting back to his room, because it was near lunchtime. I told George that we were going to get him out of there as soon as we could. How we were going to do this I didn't know, but I knew it was going to be done. By the time we left, he was the George I knew.

We did Astreas all the way home to cut George free of those surroundings. The next day I told Mother what it was like down there. She made her own calls for George at some point. Later we got a call from George saying that his son had built a ramp for his wheelchair to get up to the door of his mobile home. George was the owner of the mobile home park and was so grateful to be able to be home.

It was maybe a year later that Mother called Camelot from Montana and asked me to get all the staff into our large chapel, including all the schoolchildren. She was going to make an announcement, and she wanted everyone there. About half an hour later she called in, and they had her on a loudspeaker. First thing she asked was whether everyone was there, and there was a resounding "yes." She said that George Lancaster had ascended at such and such time, and the whole chapel was standing up and cheering. It was quite a scene. It's nice to have friends who have completed their final journey in life from the physical plane.

Working with Mother and witnessing her leadership was always rewarding. When I was out of alignment, Mother was always right on with the correction, thank goodness. I would like to relate one incident that occurred. We were to gather all the permanent staff members including all the probationary staff newly accepted as permanent staff. So here we were all gathered together. Mother was displeased about something and was giving me a stern message from the podium. I was concentrating on what I was doing, and I knew I would really mess up if I didn't continue. However, I was nodding my head yes to let her know I agreed with her. Later I asked Diana what Mother was trying to convey to me, and Mother was right as usual. We did get the job done. You might call it life in the fast lane!

Mother's staff was responsible for holding the balance for her 24 hours a day, with a system of tags that included all kinds of calls and decrees for Mother's protection. Usually the tag was a two-hour slot with at least three people from permanent and probationary staff. Mother could not do the job she was doing without this special help throughout the day and night. It was our job to know what the energy was at the time. Often Mother would call and tell us what seemed to be impinging upon her personally. She was extremely sensitive about what was going on around the planet. Sometimes we increased the tags for certain situations. At one time we had ten taggers in each slot, and that was pretty extreme.

Mother often told us about her experiences in other embodiments, including some of her mistakes. She had made bad karma from time to time that she had to make up for. There were other embodiments in which she was sainted. One was Saint Clare of Assisi and another Saint Catherine of Siena. Both were very remarkable embodiments. I did have the opportunity to read some books about Clare and Catherine. They were not easy embodiments, and the times were devastating. It was definitely the Dark Ages. They needed a saint around.

Once while Mother was at La Tourelle, she was badly burned by some hot water that spilled on her arm. Mark told her that it was karma from an embodiment in France. Her uncle had reprimanded her for something she did. He happened to own a number of village huts, and Mother was so angry that she went to the village and burned down the straw huts. Mark told her that it was heavy-duty karma and that a burn on her arm was minor. The reason it was minor was because she had aligned herself with God and had been doing his work for the ages since that embodiment. Some of her previous embodiments of worthiness did allow her the privilege to grow in grace while in the physical.

We had lots of new students and staff at Camelot. Diana and I discovered we had so much paperwork to do that we needed another secretary. Jacklyn Stratton [Daniel] joined us with her talents. Then we had a real special volunteer to help with the paper shuffling. Her name was Esta Buckland. She loved to volunteer, so we took her on. She was quite a little worker, and she was no dummy, either—she'd figure things out for herself. She was a special jewel. They all were.

Esta eventually moved to Montana with us. A little aside regarding Esta: On May 21, 2005, we celebrated her 97th birthday. She was a little on the fragile side but her mind was as sharp as a tack. She passed away on March 4, 2006.

In the early eighties, my mother decided to move to an assisted-living facility that also had its own hospital care unit. I was able to go back to Minnesota a few times to see her. Our strained relationship after my sudden departure for AMU ended with peace and calm, and we kept in touch by phone.

In 1982 I was contacted by my brother John telling me that my mother had had surgery due to a colon cancer. He said he didn't think it looked good and I should come up as soon as possible. When I arrived at the hospital my mother was extremely groggy from the painkillers and there was very little communication. I did hold her hand and talk to her. Often I went downstairs to a little chapel and prayed for her healing and recovery. It was soon time for me to leave, and she was no better.

She amazingly recovered and reached the age of 90 in 1983. One day in October 1983, I was just arousing from my night's sleep when I suddenly was aware that my mother was standing near my bed smiling at me. She was radiant, in a beautiful young form clothed in white. I called out "Mother!" and she disappeared. I quickly looked at my watch and noted the time. It was 7 a.m. I could not get my brother on the phone until later, when he confirmed that she passed on about that time. They tell me that her last words were "Call my daughter." I couldn't have been more grateful to see her so happy and beautiful.

That same week I requested the opportunity to lead the ascension service, and I dedicated it to my mother. She was a wonderful mother who had a good influence on me over the years.

Troubles in Camelot

All was not well at Camelot. A man named Gregory Mull had been hired as an architect against Mother's wishes. Later he became our adversary. He placed all his burdens on our beloved Mother, who had to appear in court because of him. It was a gross injustice against the church. The opposition on Mother was overwhelming. In the end, the church had to pay a huge sum of money because of his ridiculous lies. The jury concluded that his statements were true, since we were looked down upon in the area.

Mother was right about the man, and the fiasco cost the church plenty. Gregory Mull had been an adversary in an ancient embodiment. You might say he was one of the bad guys. He did pass on shortly after the trial, and Mother was very aware that he had gone to the second death. His opportunity to come up higher was over.

One prominent staff member was very mean-spirited to

several people whom he did not care for, and I was one of them. I knew it had to be a karmic tie from the past. He was a teaching assistant at AMU in the winter of 1974, which I attended. After his classes, I would try to figure out what he was saying. He was very wordy, but there was no substance. Our sojourn as members of the staff had its disagreeable moments over the years that are really not worth mentioning. He was totally impolite to me, and I figured that was his problem.

Lanello gave a dictation in which he dismissed this person from staff in a gracious manner. Later Mother called me into her office and told me that he and his family would be moving out of their apartment soon. He and his wife had five small children. Mother wanted me to personally do an exorcism in the apartment after their departure.

Exorcisms are a common practice in the Catholic Church. They are used to clear demons and discarnates from individuals as well as from buildings. This ritual is accomplished by placing sea salt and green long-needle pine on pieces of paper in an iron skillet. When you light the paper the combination gives off smoke. The smoke flushes out the entities and discarnates.

It was a little unprecedented to do an exorcism alone. However, Mother gave me instructions on what to do and various calls to make for a clearance. The power of the spoken Word does clear the area of dark spirits that gather around those who are dark in spirit. I made the calls and cleared all the rooms, the corners and the closets, and I shut the apartment door for 24 hours.

He and his family had moved to housing in the area. Not too long after, Mother told me that she wanted me to invite him to the conference that was coming up shortly. She explained that she wanted me to help him and escort him around. I was somewhat puzzled about this, but I obeyed immediately. I arranged to meet him at the conference. Mother wanted to make sure that he had everything he needed in new books and Summit Lighthouse materials.

We met and had a very pleasant chat. I made him feel comfortable and he made me feel comfortable. The entire meeting was very cordial. That was the last time I had any contact with him. I knew I had had heavy karma with this man someplace down the line in life. Much later, I realized that Mother was giving me the opportunity to help balance my karma with him at that time—and perhaps she was giving him the same opportunity.

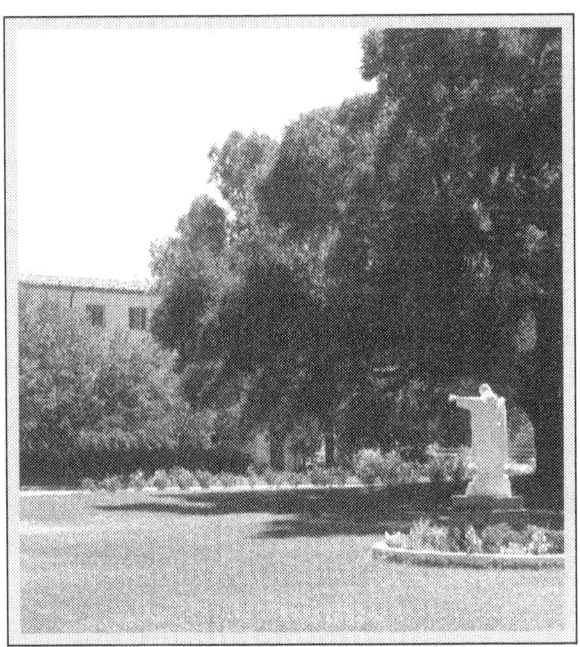

The statue of Jesus and the Rose Garden

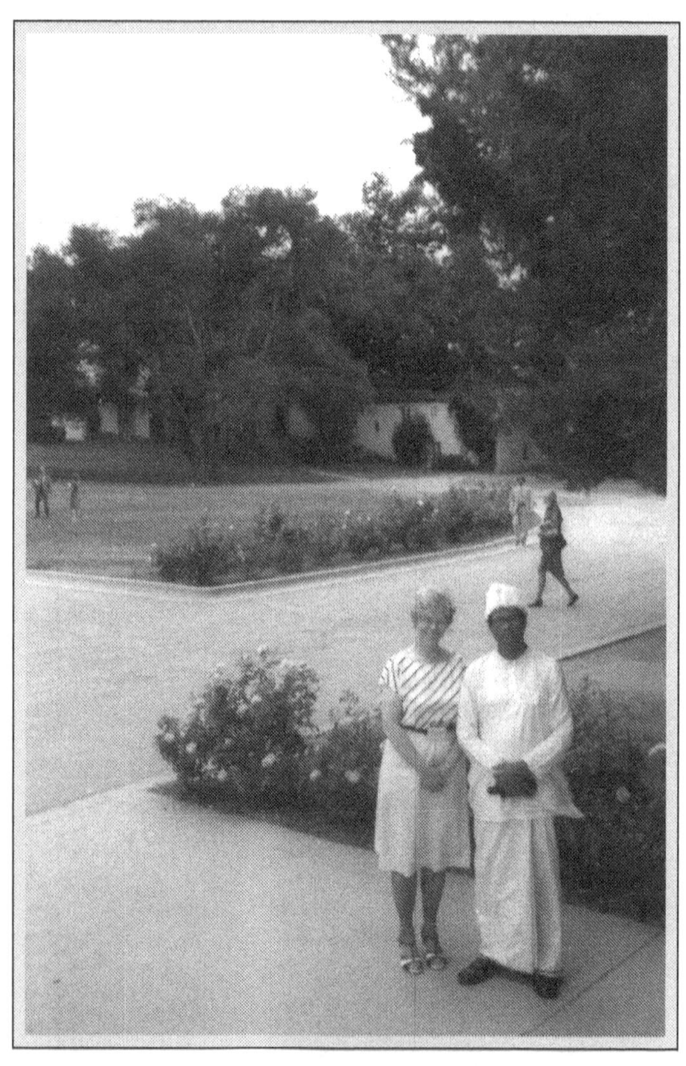

With a visitor at Camelot, 1985 (background: the Mansion)

Camelot: Closing Years

Through the years at Camelot and beyond, I kept the tags going 24 hours a day, with the help of the permanent and probationary staff. Mother by this time had married Edward Francis. They had moved to suburbia with the children. The tags never ceased, and we now had to travel to the house when Mother was there. There were usually two or three people assigned to a session. However, more might be called on if the energies were overwhelming. There was a lot of anger from the orthodox churches and little respect for our church because we were considered a cult. Yes, I would call it the cult-ure of the Divine Mother. It is the culture and love for all who struggle for Truth and know it not.

Our personnel department worked together for about five years. At that time Marilyn Barrick concluded her stay at La Tourelle and returned to Camelot to take over the personnel office. That gave me a breather to continue my work on the phones, tags, housing assignments and decree leaders.

At one point Mother formed the first group of elders, and I was part of that group. She was not inclined to have us on specific duties. We met together over situations and gave Mother our conclusions.

We had purchased the Inner Retreat in Montana in 1981, and our first conference there was held in the summer of 1982. From then on, our conferences really flourished. I was able to attend a few of them, but often I remained at Camelot to help hold the balance and to help others with things that needed to be done there. During conferences at the Inner Retreat, those of us who stayed behind were in the Chapel of the Holy Grail listening to replays of previous dictations by the same Masters who were scheduled to dictate at the Inner Retreat. The current class tapes were sent by mail as soon as possible. How quickly new innovations do appear. Now we are heard all over the world via the Internet, and everyone is on the same page.

It was not long afterward that I was asked to plan a move for our housing to a place called Hidden Trails, not too far from Camelot. They were all-purpose dorms used for a variety of activities in the area. But they fit our needs for the time being. It wasn't exactly the Ritz, but it was a dorm-like situation. "They" wanted me to put so many in a dorm, but I felt we could not allow ourselves to be overcrowded. I didn't tell them what I did when they added an extra person, I just didn't go with the program. There was a very nice house that accommodated some of our people, and it was pretty decent housing. What they didn't know didn't hurt them. As I mentioned, this camp was called "Hidden Trails." Many of us called it "Hidden Trials," and they weren't so hidden.

Before the year was out, we were placed in a complex

that was very nice, with suites to accommodate four people. They consisted of two bedrooms and a living area, which fit our egos a bit better.

Unfortunately, we did not endear ourselves to the manager. Due to our crazy hours, we had to move in late at night. We tried to be quiet, but it was almost impossible not to make noise. I could feel the undertone of the manager's attitude toward us, and I humbly went to her apartment as soon as I could to apologize. She was a little indignant, and I did try to make amends for disturbing the peace. We just chatted for a while. She mentioned that she had a hearing problem in one of her ears that had bothered her for several years. I remembered reading that hearing loss had been helped when a few drops of Swedish bitters were applied directly into the ear. I played the long shot and mentioned it to her and told her where she could purchase the bitters. About a week later she caught up with me and told me that the bitters had really helped. I truly believe that the Holy Spirit had inspired me, and she received the blessing. She got along with our group from then on and we were friends.

Slowly we were moving out of Camelot, and I was transferred around a bit in the final stages of working there. I was now answering the phone at Joyous Isle several miles from Camelot, where a lot of our staff worked. In February of 1987, Linda Terry [Worobec] and I were asked to be prepared to fly out in two days for our final move from Camelot. I was a bit shocked, but the church had two plane tickets that had to be used. It wasn't easy to pack everything we owned to be out of there in two days—one day to pack and the other day to catch a flight to Montana. We took the basics of what we needed to use right away, and the rest of the baggage came along later. It was a tough two days, but we made it.

We arrived at the Ranch and settled down the best we could with what we had. Because of all the pressure and running around, I caught a cold. A staff member mentioned that a trip to Boiling River would cure it in no time. I thought it was a good idea. So in the middle of the winter, we went to the Wyoming side of the state line, where the river was boiling hot. I got in a comfortable spot where the cold water and hot water were a good mix. Not long after, I discovered that my head was quite clear and I was back on track.

Moving Up

At the Inner Retreat with Mother, 1991

The Inner Retreat

$\mathcal{I}$t felt great to be back in the Rockies again (from a different vantage point). It reminded me so much of Colorado. We were now called the Royal Teton Ranch. I settled into the personnel department again under someone else, and of course the next assignment was housing. Another person was on the phones at that time. We were still operating a 24-hour phone service. Eventually that became another part of my job description again, including tags for Mother. It was a pretty good juggling act, because more people were coming to the Ranch and the staff was swelling as we expanded our endeavors to ranching and farming.

We had a big piece of land a few miles out of Livingston. It had very rich soil, a beautiful ranch house and a huge barn. We had farmers who tilled the soil and a large barn that housed chickens. We called it North Ranch. The ranch house was a very lovely building with three ladies who hosted guests and ranch hands as well. These ladies were the backbone of North Ranch: Grace Johnson, Esta Buckland (our little secretary from Camelot), and Celeste Huelat. They always had the best food on the table, and they always shared with the many who happened to drop in.

The church also rented a large warehouse in Livingston that was part of the old Livingston railroad yard. It was 50 miles from the Royal Teton Ranch. Here we had the graphics department, with printing presses for the many books that needed to be published. It was a pretty good-sized operation, and the people needed housing. Fortunately the church was able to lease a mobile home park with many trailers very close to North Ranch. It was called Big Spur Campground. We purchased yellow school buses to accommodate people working in Livingston and at the Ranch. When all the dust settled we had 700 staff, not counting the children.

In the early stages of our arrival we were not welcomed to the area, and there were serious problems with the locals. Again we were classified as a cult. The newspapers out of Livingston and Bozeman thrived on church-bashing articles. There were some local yokels from Gardiner, most likely from the many bars, who liked to pick a fight as some drunks will do. With the encouragement they got from the papers, they thought we could be run out of town.

We experienced an example of their rage during a New Year's conference. The session let out after midnight, and the bus for Big Spur was headed down the highway for home. Apparently a Gardiner man recognized our bus. He took a pot shot at it with his pistol as he passed by. It was aimed to do harm to someone and it did break the window. It apparently ricocheted off something, and one of the women felt it go through her hair. Fortunately no harm was done except a shattered window and some pretty scared staff.

There were careless shootings of our mailboxes about 75 times. Once a bunch of wild drunks came from Gardiner and put up a wooden cross on the edge of our property and set it on fire. It was very dry at the time. Fortunately we got the fire out before there was any damage. Graffiti was everywhere, with their foul language. They even advertised a shooting club where you got so many points for knocking out the ones in the highest positions in the church. They went so far as to put nails on the road to flatten the tires of conferees going to the conference site. The local authorities never caught up with them, and I don't think they wanted to because there was so much church-bashing. Somehow they felt we were a threat to the larger community.

However, we must practice what we have been taught and extend love to all. Love is the ultimate key, and it *is* what makes the world turn. The newspapers kept up their bigger sales for a while, but we finally got off the front page. Even now, if they can find a juicy tidbit to write about us you can bet your boots they will. We are mainstream news! But I would like to add that our relationship with Gardiner has bloomed and grown. All my contacts with the Gardiner people were great, and I liked to do business there as much as I could. The Ranch and Gardiner are working together for the greater good. Not long ago, several Gardiner people joined together as a group and met with some Ranch staff to see if we could help one another. Patience, time and love on both sides brought us together.

Most of our housing was purchased from a community of people who were closing down their operation in the northwest part of the United States. It was a fast way to get housing to accommodate us for the need of the hour. Mother wanted us to make plans for our own homes. That idea was short-lived, for one year after our move (in 1988), Mother was instructed by Saint Germain to build shelters for our safety. It was an expensive insurance policy for protection against natural disasters and possible wars. Mother obeyed immediately and got the job done. The shelters were extensive and expensive and can hold hundreds of people. It was a huge project that kept many of the men working steadily for quite some time. These units are very deep in the ground. The facilities are divided into separate units of housing, yet connected with one another, and they have all the accoutrements and conveniences necessary to function properly.

One day in 1990 the call came for the staff to move up to the shelters for the night. We found out later why Mother sounded the alarm. In the meantime, we were up most of the night using the power of the Word (decrees) to avert any impending danger. The next morning we were free to go back to our housing.

One staff member saw Mother coming out of the shelter, heading for her car. Mother was ecstatic over the fact that we had accomplished our goal of moving up to the shelters, as a test of our will to do so. We were all tired, and the staff member was amazed at Mother's exuberance. We later found out that there had been a critical situation between India and Pakistan that was averted. We needed to be tested on responding to the call to move quickly and get to our shelters ASAP. It was our first and last test, and all went well. The other part was that there were so many of us using the power of the Word in decrees that we were apparently able to hold the balance for that serious world situation.

Because of Mother's great awareness, by the grace of the Masters, of what was going on around the planet, once in a while I would get a call from Mother in the middle of the night, asking me to get everyone to King Arthur's Court ASAP for decrees. My first reaction was to get people up to help me knock on the various doors situated all over the property and sound the alarm to get to the Court. "Obey immediately" is the byword. We always responded and moved quickly into action when we heard that the power of the Word was needed by the Masters and heavenly hosts to turn a situation around.

The power of the spoken Word is the backbone of this organization. We are a different kind of army, in which the instrument is the Word in action for the armies of heaven to use. You may know that when an army comes to a bridge they cannot march across in step. They have to break ranks and walk randomly. When the group is together it is powerful enough to collapse the bridge. This is an analogy, but the same effect is seen with the power of the Word. With a large group of people, it is powerful when it is sent with love. It is a two-way street and the reverse can happen—people with an evil intent can be very destructive. However, they have no power unless by fear you give them power. Thoughts are also very powerful. They can make you or break you.

About 1992, there were several lawsuits designed to intimidate the church with false accusations. Mother talked to me about doing a round of decree 33.00, repeated 33 times. It is a Ruby Ray call that covers much of the abuse on the planet. I took the challenge and got about 45 people convinced to help with this situation. It was to be on a Monday night, which is the pink-ray day. The pink was now going to have a lot of ruby with it. I had two good decree leaders, and I had it taped. We did it in about two and a half hours.

The next day I went by Mother's office and told her how

well it went and that there was a good showing of people. She was pleased and then she added that we needed to do this every Monday night. Somehow I survived the suggestion and after a deep breath I said, "Okay, Mother, we will do what you have asked." So every Monday night we had our sessions of Ruby Ray calls. Quite a few people stayed with the program for a year or two. The numbers got down to about two or three of us, and the last year it was just me. Then they told me that the Court was going to be used on Monday nights. I really enjoyed doing it and I had a great momentum on it. At this time I still do at least one Ruby Ray call every day. I can truly say that it has had a profound effect on my spiritual growth.

Community Life

Our conferences are always special and a great joy of the gathering of the elect. We have so many backgrounds and cultures, but we are of one body and one mind to turn the world around from the burden of the "fallen ones" that has been placed upon the good people of the planet. They are the heartless ones who want to steal our light because they have none. Unfortunately, they *can* steal our light because of our inharmony, and we are the losers. Trust in the Lord God. He brings his judgments upon them according to his will and our will to offer our prayers and decrees to him. "Vengeance is mine; I will repay, saith the Lord."

Our July conferences in the Heart of the Inner Retreat were always a huge success. It took many volunteers to make them successful. Our sales tents alone were a big enterprise and worth all the effort. The big tent where Mother gave her lectures and the dictations from the Masters held at least

2,500 people. There were several tents with speakers who translated the lectures and dictations into other languages. The meal tent always had overhead speakers for the main program. We had hundreds of people, including staff and volunteers, to help with all kinds of services: setting up the tents, providing food, driving buses, taking guard duty, staffing the children's area and the nursery area, and so on. It was a bustling tent city. We had a major parade on the Fourth of July. It was always outstanding because people from all over the world participated, carrying the flag of their country and often wearing national costumes. The Heart was and still is a lovely spot, with its streams and vast mountainous areas that can be seen by hiking up the mountains. One of the best mountains to climb is Maitreya's Mountain, and there are guided hikes during the conferences.

The July conference still offers each of us the opportunity to meet our brothers and sisters from all over the world. The major activities are held in King Arthur's Court at Ranch Headquarters. On the Fourth of July we journey to the Heart for a special picnic and to enjoy the scenery.

We had our moments with the government. For a while they were checking our accounting books. This was tantamount to harassment. It took a while for the attacks to level off.

A little history about the Cinnabar Store, which we purchased and renamed: When we first arrived here, it was owned and operated by Sonny Brogan, an old-timer in the area. He maintained a bar and restaurant along with a buffalo ranch. He was quite a character.

One day I happened to be talking to him and I remembered the name Sonny Brogan. I was eleven years old (some 50-plus years before) and living in Minneapolis. Our family was invited out to a restaurant in St. Paul. The entertainment was a dinner band led by a Sonny Brogan. I remembered the name and I asked Mr. Brogan if he was that band leader. He looked pretty shocked at the question. He was really surprised that I remembered him, but he seemed very pleased. What a small world we live in. The Brogans eventually became good neighbors with us. Sonny has since passed on.

The Cinnabar Store was up for sale when we first arrived, and the church acquired it. The kitchens in the back were quickly pressed into service for our first conference in the Heart. Later it was turned into a restaurant called The Ranch Kitchen, which served up great food and entertainment for several years. Then it became a store, named The Four Winds after a health food store and restaurant that Mark and Mother ran in Colorado Springs.

For about ten years, we had a community Thanksgiving dinner in the big dining room behind the store. We asked people to call and let us know how many were coming, and to bring a dish. I would get the calls, since I was on the phones anyway, and I would try to even out the menu and make suggestions for what to bring. The staff baked the turkeys in the kitchens. It was always a big success—people came from as far away as Bozeman. It was amazing how we always had enough to feed everyone, even when extra people showed up at the last minute without contributing food. They were always welcomed. We would even have food left over for people to take home.

In this year of 2007, the restaurant has been reopened. That's an interesting story. A couple in the church, Michael and Charlene Kaufman, ran several businesses of their own, including jewelry sales and restaurants, in various locations.

Their culinary capabilities are the best. Wherever their restaurants have been, they are top-of-the-line.

The Kaufmans had owned a cabin in Glastonbury for years and decided to settle down here. For a year my friend Peggy Keathley, who's a real estate agent, looked all over Paradise Valley (which runs between Gardiner and Livingston) for a piece of land for them to purchase to build a restaurant. Occasionally Peggy would point out some lots that were ridiculous in price. But then I received a phone call from Charlene telling me that Michael had died suddenly from a heart attack. I couldn't have been more surprised by the news.

Not long after, I had a dream regarding Michael. When I woke up the next morning I knew something was on my mind about Michael, but I couldn't pinpoint it. Suddenly it came to me in a flash to tell Charlene about The Four Winds, which was being renovated. I immediately called and told her of my dream. That's all it took, and she came up to make plans to take over.

At this writing Charlene and her son, a great chef from the Los Angeles area and tops in the culinary arts, have opened their restaurant. They have done a beautiful job and have established a very nicely designed restaurant with excellent food. I think this part of Paradise Valley will be very popular one of these days. I had always hoped that they could name the restaurant The Lighthouse and put up a lighthouse to attract the tourists, and they did just that. My dream has come true, and the restaurant is called The Lighthouse.

A Conclusion

Wayne had remarried within a year or so after I left. I had met his new wife while Wayne and I were still married, though I didn't know her well. I had not been in touch with Wayne for a good many years. I did correspond with his sister Erma and with his daughter, Kathy, who had moved to Wichita. I had always hoped that Kathy would come out to see me in Montana, but it never worked out.

During the early stages of my work with the Ruby Ray calls, Erma contacted me about Wayne's physical disabilities with his neck and his arms from an old football injury and his many years of hard physical work. I was quite concerned, and I felt I needed to write him a letter asking his forgiveness for having left the way I did. For the sake of just mentioning the situation I will add it to this epistle. It is part of the process of learning, accepting, compassion and forgiveness. It is one of the beautiful episodes of my life.

December 5, 1992

Dear Wayne,

This is a letter to greet you in the spirit of inspiration and understanding on my part and understanding on your part.

Last week I called Erma because I was concerned about Kathy. For the past year I had written and called her by phone to no avail. Erma explained Kathy's situation to me. Understandably, she has been under a great burden. We had a nice chat about the past illness of her [Erma's] husband and his recovery. She told me about her son Tom, who has quite a cross to bear with the disease of MS. She also explained to me that you were having difficulty with some physical problems.

How quickly we discover that life is quite short and tenuous. The rosebud that blossoms into its cycles of beauty and exudes its sweet essence soon fades and falls to the ground.

But, unlike the rose, the soul of a man has the greatest potential to blossom and remain eternal, which is the sweeter essence of the goal of immortality. That sweeter essence is willed by the Father of all life.

As you know, I have always been a confirmed believer in reincarnation. What a great way to settle one's account for the past mistakes and errors we have made in past lives. The opportunity to clean the slate—and the soul has the ability to go higher and higher, until you are fully aware of the consciousness of God and immortal life. Who is to say we cannot traverse the cosmos in bodies celestial?

Live life to the fullest and have nothing but the strong desire to live each day as best as you know how. We are all working on misqualified energy of the past lives not lived to the best of our ability. All is opportunity, all is a learning process that leads one to a path of greater understanding and a greater awareness of what life is all about.

So comes the time the old model (the rusty body) must pass away, only to be taken up someplace down the line in the process of eternity. At some point there is the awakening of true understanding of the real nature of the soul. God endowed us with this nature, and it is the great scheme of the mystery of life.

Just wanted to let you know that I have great compassion for your soul, including all souls who walk the earth. I also wanted to express my gratitude to you for being a great teacher of fortitude and your desire to push on when the going gets tough. During those many years of hunting we enjoyed together, I acquired a greater understanding of that endurance that you so aptly expressed over the years.

You have been a very active man physically that not even the younger men could outdo. However, the time comes when one must look for inner strength and inward endurance. It is time to reflect the inner knowings and the inner sowings that set the sails for a greater impetus to come.

Prepare yourself for greater knowledge as you prepared yourself, as a youth, to become an excellent pilot that earned your wings. Search for those pinions of light, reach for the stars, they are there to be traversed. This message is not to open a chapter but to close it graciously, hopefully sealing this message with true understanding.

It is my desire that you hold no ill will toward me for my leaving so suddenly. It was time for me to go to be free to search for another part of me that was aching to be found.

—Jean

It was not long afterward that, to my astonishment, I received a package from Wayne. In the package was *Men Who Fly*, the book that he had published about his experiences as an airline captain. I had hoped that writing this story and getting it all out would help him to deal with the situation emotionally. He was working on this book on the oil rig, and he took his trusty typewriter to the job while drilling at the same time. He knew when he had to check the line and did so frequently. I took some pictures of him in this mode, quite interesting.

It was late in the evening when I discovered the package with the completed book. I was truly shocked to have the book in my hands. When I opened it, I found a message in the preface addressed to me in very shaky handwriting from Wayne. I began to peruse the book for about an hour. To my great astonishment, I was included throughout the book. Later on I was able to delve into the text. Naturally, to make the story interesting, flowing and readable, Wayne had exaggerated some details. The most beautiful part of the book was his handwritten statement in the preface, which brought tears to my eyes.

From then on until Wayne passed away about four years later, I kept writing him encouraging letters. He could not respond because he became more incapacitated as time went on. His wife wrote me letters to let me know how he was doing, to the final point when he had to be hospitalized.

The day of his passing was quite interesting. It was the day of a wedding, and I had been asked to stand in as the mother of the groom. It was a Saturday and there was very little activity at the Ranch. I was walking through a large eating area. No one was around, and no one knew I was there. There was a table with a phone on it, and just as I got to the table the phone rang, right on cue. To say the least the place was empty, and I couldn't imagine the operator placing the call there. I picked up the phone and it was Wayne's sister Erma telling me that Wayne had just passed on. I was so grateful that she had called me, but on an extension? That was a shock!

I never figured out how I got that call, but it gave me the opportunity to be in the chapel where I could quietly make my calls for Wayne's passing. I could definitely feel his presence. This is one time I truly felt the angels of heaven working little miracles.

I've always loved Wayne and been concerned for him. I don't know when I first learned about twin flames—probably at AMU. I've wondered ever since if Wayne and I were twin flames. But sometimes even twin flames can't be together for some reason. I asked Mother one time if Wayne was my twin flame, and she said she couldn't tell me.

With Dorothy Lee Fulton

Messenger of Music

At this time in my story I would like to reflect back on our Messenger of Music, Dorothy Lee Fulton, who has been guided by Mother Mary throughout the years to write heaven's music.

I was at the Motherhouse in 1974 when Dorothy Lee married Milton Fulton. Mother performed the ceremony. It was a small wedding and it gave me the opportunity to introduce myself to her. That meeting eventually would give me a lifelong friend, whom I would meet again.

Dorothy Lee came to Camelot, where she worked with the choir and continued receiving the heavenly music. She was Mother's personal confidante and friend, as was Mother her personal confidante and special friend.

In 1982 a few of the staff started the move to the Ranch, and in 1987 it became the final destination for all of us. In the early nineties, Milton passed on and Dorothy Lee soon came to join us. She rented a small apartment in Gardiner, where she continued bringing forth the special music that she produces so prolifically. This music is her total life, and she is absorbed in it unflinchingly. Dorothy Lee and I became fast friends, and I had the opportunity every Saturday to tidy up for her and do her laundry. I made sure she had a good meal that day, and we enjoyed each other's company. I tried to keep a list of all her music at that time, and she has since surpassed that.

Dorothy Lee's next move was to a big house near the Sphinx mobile home park, which she shared with a couple of ladies at that time. It was there that we had a big shower for Mother before the birth of Seth. It was a great occasion and an opportunity to see old friends.

Dorothy Lee received loving recognition in a dictation given by Mother Mary, who is the standard-bearer for the heavenly hosts who work with Dorothy Lee. Dorothy Lee's devotion to the Blessed Mother is expressed in the many statues and pictures around her home.

Her last move was to South Glastonbury, to a house that overlooks the beautiful valley and a range of scenic mountains. Every week she calls her choir together to practice the old music or to record the new. The music stirs the soul and takes you on a flight to the higher realms of consciousness. It moves the spirit into the power of God that is within us.

At this time (2007) Dorothy Lee is 93 years old. We are very fortunate that she is still very capable of doing heaven's work on earth, not only for our generation but for generations to come.

Changes

*J*n 1994 and 1995, El Morya encouraged the staff to go out and pursue further education. Because of the growing technologies, we needed to be up to date. Saint Germain has said that further technologies will come forth when mankind is ready. At this time in history, I can imagine that a lot is being held back because of irresponsible groups and the immorality that is attempting to take hold of society. Mankind needs to grow in grace and harmony. We need to do the best we can to interact with one another gracefully to get important jobs done.

Our Internet broadcasts are capable of reaching around the world for our spiritual decree work that makes us one big family. With all the teaching centers and study groups, we can work together to make a difference in the serious issues of church and state. Some former staff members settled in teaching centers across the nation, got jobs and support the teaching centers.

Mother gave birth to her fifth child, Seth, at the age of 55, and I am sure it took a toll on her physical body. Not too long after that she and Edward Francis divorced. Her other children had scattered across the United States. In 1998, she began to pull back from a lot of her duties and placed others in positions of authority. At that point the new leaders began to downsize the employees. They stopped the tags, as they couldn't see any reason for them. That is when Mother really hit bottom, with no support system whatsoever. She had and still has a heavy mantle that she will always carry.

By the grace of God, Judy Sue Christenson picked up the torch and has a worldwide tag going for Mother night and day. Many of us are taggers and will continue to tag, for the love that Mother has given to each one of us.

Travels with Peggy

*P*eggy Keathley and I have been good friends for a long time. She and I were on staff together for many years. Before that, Peggy lived on Maui, where she ran a successful real-estate business. When she became a Keeper of the Flame, she set up a seminar for Mother on Maui. She was so impressed with Mother that in 1975 she came for three months to attend Summit University at La Tourelle. At the end of that time, she joined staff.

In 1992 Peggy invited me to join her on a trip to Hawaii. I had so much fun picking up shells of all different shapes and sizes. I brought a box full of them home and made all kinds of objects out of them, which I sold when we had a church bazaar. It was a fundraiser for the church. Various staff members and Keepers of the Flame joined in the bazaar. Everything imaginable was presented. It was in King Arthur's Court and many booths were set up offering all kinds of diverse

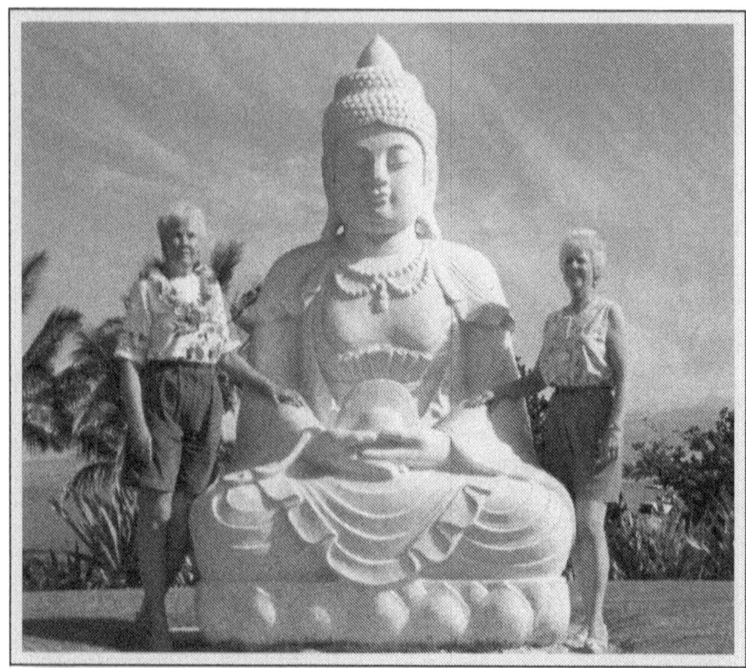

Peggy, Kuan Yin and me, 1992

items. It was quite a success.

In the spring of 2006, Peggy and I went back to Hawaii again. We rented a car and spent a lot of time in the high mountains of Maui, as well as on the beaches looking for shells and in the water, snorkeling.

About 1999 Peggy asked me to make a trip with her to teaching centers and study groups to promote her project for Avalon, a proposed assisted-living facility for the elderly in Emigrant, Montana. There will be separate little apartments with all the conveniences, including a small kitchen. Peggy wants each resident to have one major meal each day served in a large dining area, which will provide full nutritional meals. It is a project near and dear to her heart, and she is still working at this time for it to be completed.

I fortunately was able to get a leave of absence from staff. Our reason for the trip was to make everyone aware that this project would be available in the future for all who would be interested at some time in their life. Avalon is in a beautiful setting and near enough for regular trips to town as needed.

We planned to travel to Kansas, Missouri, Oklahoma and Texas. We would arrive during the day, present the program in the evening and then leave the next day. Texas was a big chunk, and we planned to stop at several places in that state. Our next stops would be along the Gulf coast and up the east coast to New York City. From New York we would cross over into Detroit, contacting study groups. Our next major stop would be at Chicago. Our final stop would be Minneapolis, and then back to Montana.

It looked good on paper. The next step was to get a vehicle that could meet all our needs. Peggy had the funds to purchase an RV. We made many a trip to Bozeman to find the right vehicle that was affordable and easy to drive. That last part was important because we needed practice in driving a larger vehicle.

We soon had the problem solved except for Peggy's two cats, Himalaya and her offspring Kuthumi. That is when Peggy asked me if we could take them. I was a bit dubious at first, but of course I knew we had to. Peggy and the cats are very attached to each other—except that Himalaya has no attachment to Kuthumi.

We were off and all things were going well as far as our timing and seeing the study groups. We got to Texas. Unfortunately, Peggy spotted a museum and thought we had plenty of time to stop and take a look. It was all very interesting until we were walking around a large statue that had a broad base and sharp corners, which Peggy hit with her leg. It was a deep cut, and it bled profusely. We cleaned it and bandaged the wound. I wanted to get her to a doctor to have it stitched, which I knew it needed, but Peggy was concerned about the time and wanted to go on.

Of course she had a lot of pain in that leg, and it was now up to me to do the driving. Peggy became the official navigator and map checker. Driving has always been easy for me, but unfortunately the trip was just getting started. There was a lot of territory to cover. There happened to be a doctor along our route who was a Keeper of the Flame and had his own study group. He gave Peggy some antibiotics to check any infection. The leg was pretty tender, and many times she put her leg up on the dash.

The trip along the coast was great. All the little groups greeted us with open arms and plenty of food. The only time I really blew it was when we got to Virginia Beach near where the Reichardts live. We were on what seemed to be a major five-lane highway, in a lot of traffic. I was driving and Peggy was directing our course. We were in the third lane and we were within a few blocks of turning off.

Unfortunately, however, this driver was not aware that she needed to switch to the reserve tank when the gas gauge got down to empty. The only time you can switch to your reserve tank is when the vehicle is moving. I had been so intent on maneuvering through traffic that I had failed to make the switch. We found ourselves rolling to a dead stop in the middle lane, with traffic zipping by us on both sides. Suddenly an ambulance pulled up behind us, and the guy jumped out and said, "Don't get out of your vehicle, ladies"—which we were not about to do, anyway. Peggy was on her cell phone about that time, and soon a patrol car appeared. They helped us get to the side of the road and gave us some gas. They were very gentlemanly and very kind. That scenario never happened again. We had a great time with the Reichardts, who have a lovely place facing a lagoon with beautiful trees all over their backyard.

We soon were on our way to New Jersey to seek out Charlotte Mizzi in her very lovely duplex on a busy street. She was a great hostess and she provided us with terrific meals. We parked the RV on a side street where it was less noisy and we slept fine. Our next stop was the New York Teaching Center, and I was not about to get into that traffic. Charlotte zipped us over in her car, and she went through the tunnel and the traffic like a pro. When she came into busy downtown Manhattan, she immediately pulled into a parking place near the Center. She said she never failed to find a parking spot. That's what I call a positive attitude. The New York Teaching Center gave us a warm welcome and asked us several questions about the project.

We wanted to go to the top of the Statue of Liberty, and Charlotte suggested we pick up a ferry on the Jersey side. Her suggestion paid off well. We were soon on the island, and so were hundreds of schoolkids. It was their day to be at the statue. We went all the way to the crown with howling schoolkids up and down over 300 steps. It was peaceful at the crown, with only a few people allowed in at one time. Ah, peace for a few minutes! The quiet was greatly appreciated, and so was the fantastic view. We braced ourselves for the downward trek and ached to have some earplugs. But the noise did not take away the beauty of the harbor or the lovely Lady herself. That was the memorable part.

We were on our way again with a few stops, including Detroit, and then we headed for Chicago. Peggy was still the navigator. We went through a tollgate and then Peggy guided me through the various highways. She called ahead for directions—and before we realized it we were approaching the same tollgate we had passed through some time before, going in the opposite direction. We got more instructions and we were back on track.

That night, Peggy's cat Kuthumi got out for about the fourth time. This time he tore the screen. About midnight Peggy discovered that he was out again. There was a lovely large backyard with a fence quite a ways from the house. The fence paralleled a highway that had a lot of traffic. We were in our nightwear moving about the lawns in the neighborhood, whispering Kuthumi's name so as not to wake anyone. About 30 minutes later I told Peggy I was going back to bed— we had a long trip the next day. She decided to wait until morning also. At daylight we checked the shrubs close to the cement wall right next to the highway, and we heard this frightened little meow. Apparently the traffic noise was his nemesis. That was Kuthumi's last outing.

Our final stop was the Minneapolis Teaching Center and we had a great time there. What a fantastic group.

Since I was so near what was once my family's home, I asked Peggy if she would mind stopping there. It was somewhat early in the morning, and we knocked at the back door. The gentleman of the house came to the back door in his pajamas. He told us later that he wondered what in the world these older ladies were selling. He invited us in and I explained who I was and that I had some history about this house they might be interested in. It wasn't too long before we were all in the living room with his wife and two young daughters. I gave them the history and they asked a lot of questions. They didn't know that Frank Lloyd Wright had helped design the house until I told them about it. We had a great interaction with these people, so much so that they came out here to Montana a couple of times. They stayed at the Chico Resort, which Peggy and I introduced them to.

Now we were on our last lap and a few hundred miles from home, and Peggy decided she could get behind the wheel again and take over the driving. I kidded her about the timing, but I didn't mind the opportunity to sit back for a while. The entire trip was a success to be able to contact so many wonderful Keepers of the Flame. We made new friends and we have a different perspective on those who hold the balance out in the field. They love to have people from the Ranch come by to see them, and they are so eager to serve you in any way they can.

In the final analysis, we traveled 8,500 miles and over only about 100 of it we got lost. We managed to stay out of trouble and had no accidents except taking the wrong road occasionally. Of course we had a few cat tales. I can't blame Kuthumi for wanting to venture out as he did.

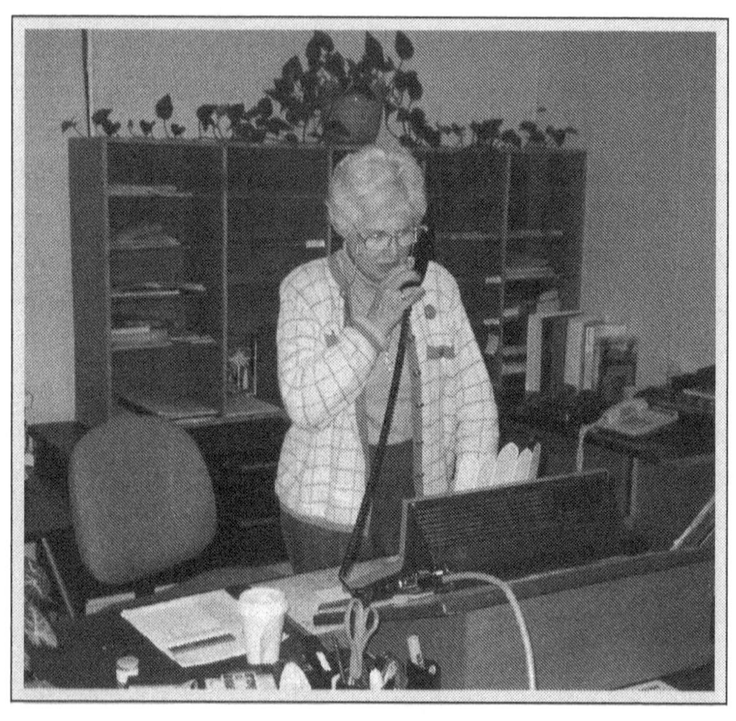

At my desk at Ranch Office

New Initiations

$\mathcal{U}$p until recently, the Ranch staff was scattered around in various buildings, which wasn't always convenient. In the spring of 2005, there was a groundbreaking ceremony for a new office building at Ranch Headquarters that would hold all of us. We moved in about a year later. It was quite a change for us to be under one roof after so many years.

My new desk was right at the main entrance. It was a lovely area, with a dual fireplace. The other side of the fireplace was in a big room that I could look into, which they used for meetings or dances or whatever they needed. Behind me were the mailboxes. I was the receptionist and the phone operator, and I sorted the mail.

I was always so grateful to work on the phones. That position gave me time to talk to people all over the world. I took a great counseling course, and I had many opportunities to listen to people's troubles. Mainly, I called to the Holy

Spirit to help me help them walk through their problems. Just listening to people's problems gives them time to reflect on what's bothering them, and that's half the battle. Lots of help from the Holy Spirit can turn situations around. If the problem was pretty heavy-duty, I asked people to send a small picture of themselves to put on my world map. I got up at 3:30 a.m. to start my decrees for the day, and of course I saw all the faces.

Apparently, there were exorbitant expenses for the new office building, which caused a bit of a money crisis. Shortly after the building was completed, they called a staff meeting. Because I had to answer the phones, I didn't generally go to staff meetings. But that day they sent someone to take my place so I could go to the meeting. I thought, "Well, that's unusual." At the very end of the meeting, they said that they were going to have to let some staff go. I figured right then and there that I was on my way out.

My name begins with A, so I was the first one called in to be notified. They were very nice about it, very cordial. I wasn't bothered about it at all, even though I didn't know what my future would be—they were more upset than I was. I had taken maybe 50 steps from the door of the office where I had met with them, and I mentioned to someone that I wouldn't be around much longer because I had been let go. She said, "Call the Bozeman Teaching Center—the lady who lives there is moving out and they are looking for someone to take her place." So I called, and when my job at the Ranch was done at the end of August, I moved into the teaching center in Bozeman.

I have a very comfortable room upstairs. I see the sun come up in the morning. It's a lovely view. I get up at 4 a.m. now, and we start our vigil at 5 and decree from 5 to 7. I make sure that I am up on the world news to make the calls for all kinds of situations, just as Keepers of the Flame do everywhere on the planet. Other people come in for evening services and sometimes evening decrees. They have lovely services here, but I go to bed early because I get up so early in the morning. My room is right over the chapel. Fortunately, I have good earplugs.

Once they had an event here for teenagers, from Bozeman and other places. They came for two days and a night. They did a lot of games together and some studying, and they wanted me to give them a talk on Mark. I gave my talk, and they were very attentive and asked a lot of questions. And practically every one of those kids came up and gave me a big hug. It was really neat. I like those kids—they're precious. I enjoyed being with them.

I've had a lot of fun in my life, and I'm still having fun. The teaching center has a lovely wide yard enclosed by a white fence, with beautiful trees and a little stream with a bunch of ducks. The ducks had always been a little too friendly, coming up to the front of the building and making messes on the cement patio. And I thought, "This has got to change." So I started feeding them regularly, morning and evening. And they got the message real quick. They know exactly when it's feeding time. But I always go out the back door and all the way around the house, so they don't see where I'm coming from. They all get around my feet, hunting for the feed, but I make them wait until I get down to the stream. So there's no poop on the stoop any more.

I love to read the Masters' books. I don't pick anything else up—maybe a Smithsonian magazine, but that's about it. Way back in Santa Barbara, I told Mother that I had read *Climb the Highest Mountain* and that I was so thrilled. And

Mother said, "If you read it again, you'll get more out of it, because every time you read it you're on a different level of consciousness. You're absorbing one part of it, and the next time you read it you'll absorb another part. The more you read it, the more you'll understand it." So I go over and over the Masters' books, and absorb more.

My greatest opportunity has been serving the public in many diverse ways. The lesson is love of service, no matter where you are. Each day brings new interactions, testing, listening and hopefully doing the will of God.

I have learned in life to be kind and courteous to everyone, because each soul has its burden. Love the soul, because that is the key to see through the density that some people place upon themselves. Send them love instead of negative thoughts. It is such a healing balm to the soul, a ray of hope and redemption that can make a difference in the blink of an eye. Love does make a difference, and it can remove some of the baggage a soul has been burdened with. Love is truly the key. God is love, and we are all a part of God in this great adventure to become who we really are. We can help each other to find our way home to the power we have within ourselves and to our true identity in this great universe of God's kingdom. As the Bible says, "Ye are gods, and all of you are children of the Most High."

After reviewing my life through these chapters at my age of 78, I can say I have been truly blessed. Yes, there were ups and downs, but everything is a learning process. You have to have a positive attitude and learn how to be positive about anything. If it's not a good experience, it's still positive because you gain through that experience. Each soul must receive pluses and minuses in life. By the grace of God, I had many pluses, and I perceived the minuses as great lessons.

Each step of the way is a stepping stone of maturity that leads you to a wholeness and a completeness, if you look at the sunny side of life.

A negative consciousness takes you down, a positive consciousness takes you up. Everything is a growing process of the soul—weeding out negative thoughts and rising higher in consciousness on the path of becoming who you really are. This path has its stones and briars. But they are nothing when the soul is happy, casting off the darkness and looking to the light and to the God within, which is the true understanding of sons and daughters of God.

There is an alchemical change that occurs within the individual—mentally, emotionally and physically. I would add that it also depends on your own personal vibration. If you are inharmonious, the power of the light will avoid you. At that point you are not a pure instrument for God to work through. It's best to remind yourself to get back on track and make an honest appraisal of yourself if you become angry or upset, and call on the law of forgiveness. I had to go back over the years where I had held some unhappy thoughts about some people. I realized that I had held concepts of them that were incorrect because my own lack of understanding made me hold a grudge. Forgiveness of others (and of oneself first) is a lesson that we must learn in order to be on the true path.

Fortunately I was raised and influenced by wonderful parents who gave me the opportunity to grow up in the beautiful woods of Minnesota. I had swimming, fishing, hiking, sailing, hunting, and even ice skating, also the love of gardening. It was a close-knit family, which included the larger family of relatives and friends in the North Woods.

I also had the opportunity of marrying the one I loved, and I lived with him for 21 years. I hold that love dear to this day. He truly expressed that love to me years later when he published the book I encouraged him to write.

I am grateful that I made my decision to attend Ascended Master University and then to be a part of the staff and eventually our community in Montana. The teachings of the Masters implore us to come up higher. We are all working together for the divine purpose of life. We have to reach for the stars. Many of our brothers and sisters who have ascended from this activity are calling us to come up higher.

May your journey to the higher way be fulfilling and bring you many victories.

Pax Vobiscum

Renderings over a Period of Time and Space in Meditation on Maitreya

Jean Inglis Allison, 2003–2004

✠ Peace, be still, and know that wherever you are, God IS!

✠ Open the door to your higher consciousness, the Christ consciousness, and you will find those who are in need of your love, the Divine Love that can raise them up.

✠ May you know the peace that passeth understanding—share that peace of your Presence with others. Peace, be still, and know that I AM God.

✠ Life's blessings come when you open the door of your heart.

✠ Be kind, be thoughtful, be generous, and be the Word of God in action.

✠ Make every moment count.

✠ Each day is a new beginning. Let a holy action within you rise and shine.

✠ Know that compassion comes from love and understanding. Hold the balance for others so they may find the way to truth and a life with God!

✠ Hold love in you intensely for the lightbearers who have lost their way home.

✠ Kindness toward others cuts the real from the unreal. When you uphold the Christ in all through kindness and tenderness, it may help them rise up to a higher consciousness.

✠ You must first redeem yourself. Then you have the power of God within you to redeem others to come up higher in consciousness.

✠ God is the comforter of all life. Call on him daily to have the wisdom of the Holy Spirit.

✠ Know that the God-given wise ones will save the children of God through good works.

✠ The tendency to get off-balance can be ended swiftly by raising your consciousness to your higher self, the Christ Self.

✠ Move on to a higher ground in your thoughts, feelings, words and deeds.

✠ The world needs to know what steps to take so they may find the path. That path to righteousness, the right use of the Law, is the path of a chela of the will of God.

✠ When you see a destitute individual panhandling, give him some money, but also send love from your heart to the heart of that one. That's the real giving!

✠ Take dominion over all aspects of darkness. Do not allow it to enter your consciousness as a flash of thought. Out the door it goes! OM MANI PADME HUM.

✠ Instill the youth with the fiery energy of God. They must carry on the battle.

✠ In unity is our strength, in discord there is loss.

✠ Being in harmony is bliss to the soul.

✠ Hold fast that which thou hast learned.

✠ Intensify love in action when all else is chaos, and be at peace.

✠ Be at peace—your Presence is always in alignment with God. Do your work with joy and diligence.

✠ Let resolutions come through the Mind of Christ within you.

✠ Remember, count your blessings daily.

✠ Never despair, for the answer will come. When you have the faith and determination, the answer will come!

✠ Understand that God is love and compassion. If you stay the course, his guiding light will always be with you.

✠ Cease all destructive thoughts, words or deeds toward yourself and others.

✠ If you desire to be a loving and kind person, keep your heart open always to all life.

✠ The Great I AM is giving you the power to move mountains in your own world as well as the earth itself.

✠ Do not feel bereft about anything. Rise up and be a shining star to all life.

✠ Worship the Lord God with all thy heart, with all thy mind and with all thy spirit and all thy soul. Rise up to new dimensions and be an instrument. At every moment, emit that love and remain centered.

✠ Try to fulfill all your desires and dreams for God that are in your heart.

✠ Let the wonders and works of God embolden your own works as he works through you.

✠ Perfect thy words and works each day.

✠ Look for the "new dawning" of essence bright that comes from greater insight within you.

✠ Know the wisdom of God that raises one up from all human conditions.

✠ By only seeking shall you find.

✠ Be thou the all and make it known this day that you are born anew each day. All is opportunity.

✠ Be of good cheer as you live through the years and seek out the goodness of life.

✠ Be thou made whole and take dominion over self.

✠ May the children of God be blessed with wisdom each day of their lives.

✠ May you be raised up with the Mind of God vibrating in your soul.

✠ Be at peace and know that God is working through the Christ Self and a new age will appear.

✠ May you be blessed with the total understanding of the God that is within you.

✠ Know that you are worthy.

✠ Be of good cheer. Life never ends, but there are always new beginnings.

✠ Teach the children to love God and they will become God.

✠ Be gentle with self and others.

✠ Be still and know that I, Maitreya, am in all hearts that love.

✠ May God bless you with the fragrance of his love and help the weary traveler.

✠ Come into Maitreya's heart and be that loving, caring, compassionate One.

✠ My beloved, never fear of wasting time. When help is needed, give it willingly and freely.

✠ Praise God from whom all blessings flow.

✠ Dawn is that glorious time to open the heart.

✠ Move quickly each day to expand the heart flame. Do not fail to do the holy works of God.

✠ Seek out the scriptures and the teachings that are hidden in the Masters' words. They are there and you will perceive when you pursue.

✠ Be thou not burdened because life in the physical has its burdens. Help others by the power of the Word, and you help yourself.

✠ Be not deceived by the outer consciousness. Let the Christ Self and the I AM Presence tutor you in the Law daily.

✠ Be not discouraged, for the children of God must go through the dark night of the soul to reach the light of the Spirit.

✠ Know that the living Word is always in your heart, a gift from the Father to help all mankind.

✠ If you only knew of the power that is within your being, because of the Christ within, you would be astonished. Go with the Good Word each day.

✠ Do not be hurried. Be thoughtful, graceful, kindly toward self and a humanity in turmoil. Be an anchor of light.

✠ Be thou not overcome. Know the Lord seeks thee every moment and hour of the day for the world to be free.

✠ Love is the key! When you hold such love in your heart, you will have an effect on the world that can make the difference.

✠ Rise and be the sons and daughters of Zion. Master your four lower bodies.

✠ Freedom has its price, but it is worth it!

✠ Stand firm and be the holy will of God.

✠ Come! Be a chela of the will of God. Follow the Guru.

✠ Fill your mind, your heart and spirit with the Holy Spirit each day.

✠ Put others before self and make a difference in their worlds.

Be no longer burdened.
Rise up, sons and daughters, and be God!

The End